GIRL CODE

GAMING,

GOING VIRAL,

AND

GETTING IT DONE

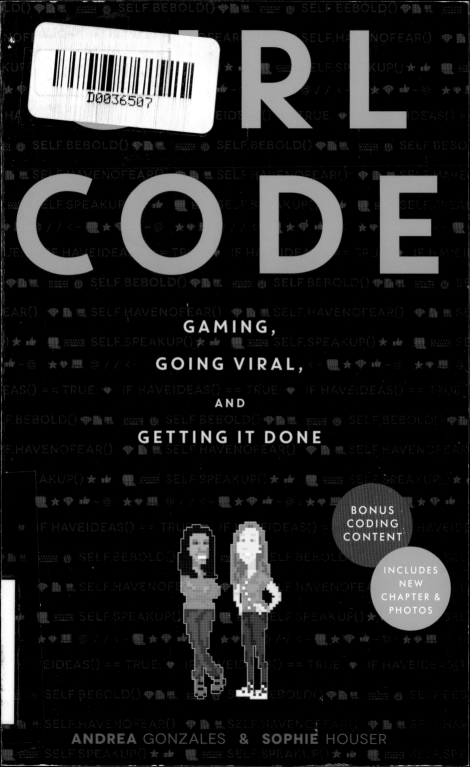

ANDREA GONZALES & **SOPHIE** HOUSER

GIRL

For Reshma Saujani, Girls Who Code, and girls who code everywhere. And also for those who want to learn— you won't regret it.

All photos used with permission of Sophie Houser and Andrea Gonzales, except for: page 221, photo by Nadia Gilbert, and page 241, photo by Stephanie Keller.

Girl Code
Copyright © 2017 by Andrea Gonzales and Sophie Houser
All rights reserved. Printed in the United States of America.

Library of Congress Control Number: 2016940932
ISBN 978-0-06-247247-2

Typography by Erin Schell
18 19 20 21 22   PC/LSCH   10 9 8 7 6 5 4 3 2 1

First paperback edition, 2018

INTRODUCTION

If you had told us that one day we would be writing a book about the time we learned to code, created a menstruation-themed video game, and then watched as that game went viral overnight and shook up our lives forever, we would have laughed in your face.

Back in 2014 we were living comfortably in our high school bubbles, having the same experiences many of you are having, worried about all the same things you're worried about. Friends, grades, romances, college . . . we were thinking about it all, too. It wasn't until we went to Girls Who Code that the bubble popped. We were flung out of our co-ed high schools and thrust into an all-girl community in a meeting room in a corporate office building in New York City, where we covered the fundamentals of coding for seven hours a day for seven weeks. We were given the tools to turn ideas that we'd only imagined into actual, functioning apps, programs, and games. Through Girls Who Code, we discovered the power of computer science and how it can inspire, mold careers, and change lives. After all, it completely transformed ours.

On September 4, 2014, we officially launched our video game, *Tampon Run*, on its own website. The game was our final project from the Girls Who Code program, and we decided we had to share it with the internet. An old-school-style side-scrolling platformer game, *Tampon Run* aims to address the social stigma against menstruation, satirizing how blood from guns and violence is more culturally acceptable than blood from periods.

As it turned out, the internet really loved it! They loved it a lot. Today, *Tampon Run* has reached more than half a million people all over the world through the original Web game and the mobile app, and we've traveled the nation talking about the gender gap in technology and the menstrual taboo.

Since the game launched, we've had time to reflect on how we've changed as people, how *Tampon Run* has evolved as a product, and how we've impacted the world. And we're still a little baffled as to how we got here. But what we know for sure is that we needed to share the story of our journey. We needed girls everywhere to know that whatever they want to do and whoever they want to be, anything is possible. Just look at us.

SOPHIE AND **ANDY**

A LITTLE BIT ABOUT SOPHIE

SOPHIE

I stared at the pages in front of me: an outline of the presentation I had to give to my eleventh-grade English class in twelve hours. I knew I needed to practice, but I couldn't. I tried to open my mouth to begin, but I couldn't. I couldn't even do the presentation for my empty bedroom. Just the *thought* of having to open up in public and share these ideas—my ideas—paralyzed me.

I got up from my desk and walked unsteadily to the dining room, where my mom was working on her computer. My stream of tears immediately got her attention. "I can't do it," I told her. "I can't."

I felt beyond angry and frustrated with myself. All I had to do was talk to a roomful of my classmates for seven minutes about *Oedipus Rex*. I had loved the play and had a lot to say about it. I loved my classmates too. How could I be so shaken by a presentation?

But I shouldn't have been surprised. I'd always had trouble openly expressing myself in school; I'd always been the quiet one in class. My report cards from over the years say it all:

Class: Tudor England (History)
Spring 2011, 8th grade
A great report despite your reluctance to present it aloud. (Why do you always do that?)

Course: American Literature II
Winter 2012, 9th grade
Excellent work this year. You've excelled in all aspects of the course (although at the risk of sounding like a broken record I'm going to repeat that it would have been good to hear you speak up more often in class).

Course: Economic History of Globalization
Fall 2013, 10th grade
An excellent writer with a firm grasp of the subject. Too bad we heard so little from her in class.

Course: Intro to Biology
Fall 2013, 11th grade
You are off to a good start this semester. One point
that needs improvement is class participation.

It wasn't that I hadn't wanted to participate. I'd just held
myself back because I felt what I had to say was meaningless.
I believed my thoughts were stupid and anyone who heard
them would think I was stupid. I often spent my hour-long
morning subway commute mulling over past conversations
where I had said something strange, past situations where
I had acted weird. And then, late at night, when my parents were both sleeping, our large, dark apartment would
envelop me and I would get lost again in feeling inadequate
and idiotic. During those nights, I'd wonder whether I
would grow out of the feeling or whether I would be stuck
being insecure for the rest of my life. How would I have a
job and be a functional adult if I spent all my time questioning myself?

Looking back on that night in eleventh grade when I got
so worked up about a minor presentation, I feel like laughing
and giving Past Sophie a piece of chocolate and a big hug. I
wish the old me could know that when I tell people I used to
be terrified to speak up, to raise my hand and say something
in class—they don't believe me. That's because now I'm all
about speaking up and speaking out, ever since I co-created

an 8-bit video game about menstruation that went viral and completely changed my life.

Before *Tampon Run*, I was a shy, quiet girl from the Upper West Side of Manhattan. Since I was born I'd lived in the same apartment with my parents and two older brothers. I went to Bard High School Early College and I loved to ride the subway, bike around the city, take photos with my mom's old Minolta, and play tennis. I was a normal kid. A normal kid who, for the first seventeen years of her life, felt this mental and physical terror over sharing her ideas with anyone other than close friends and family. With public speaking, I felt vulnerable because I had to get the words exactly right as they came out of my mouth. There were no second chances. You opened your mouth, and the world judged. I also felt uncomfortable sharing my ideas in papers or essays or any school assignment because I considered anything graded a measure of my self-worth. I saw grades as an opportunity to A) prove my belief that I was dumb, or B) disprove my belief that I was dumb. No pressure or anything . . .

The only way I felt comfortable expressing myself was through journaling. Personal writing had long been a cathartic act for me, beginning with keeping a journal when I was young. It was a way to process my thoughts and express and understand myself better. Unlike graded exercises or public speaking, no one read or judged what I put in my journal. It was the only place I could be the person I aspired to be. The only place I could dream and muse and not have to censor or edit myself—the only place I felt confident that, one day, I had a future as someone who could share her voice.

During eleventh grade, I finally found a way outside of journaling to loosen up and to stop obsessing over whether my ideas were "smart" or "dumb." I befriended a group of girls at school who showed me it was fun to be myself and do it outwardly. They told me over and over, through their words and their actions, that my ideas were funny, good, and important to share. I discovered what a joy it was to be heard. I thought about Future Sophie, ninety-something years old and lying on her deathbed, and how disappointed old-lady me would be if I kept my ideas to myself forever. Speaking up and speaking out was the only way to affect people in this world. And what would my life be worth if nothing I did ever affected anyone?

As my friendships grew and I began to realize that I aspired to leave the world better than I found it, I formed a quiet dream of finding a way to make a real impact on others. I hoped to change humanity for the better. "Like Voldemort, but in a good way," I used to say. I didn't think I'd actually achieve greatness because, despite my newfound comfort expressing myself with my close girlfriends and my budding urge to speak up, I still couldn't even raise my hand in English class. But the dream wouldn't go away. I hated my inability to get over my insecurities. I had ideas I was excited about, so why couldn't I just say them? I longed to be heard, not only by the pages of my journal or in late-night chats with my best friends. I believed I could really be something when I grew up and, in order to accomplish that dream, I'd have to speak up.

Late one night I asked my mom if I could see a therapist. She got straight to work finding me someone great, and a few weeks later I found myself in front of a therapist I'll refer to as Dr. Graham. He was a short older guy with glasses and white wispy hair, whose laugh reminded me of the Pillsbury Doughboy's. We sat across from each other every Tuesday for forty-five minutes and I told him about my week and my friends and the mean girls from elementary school who had hurt my feelings. Dr. Graham recommended I come to one of the speaking circles his wife ran, where a small group of people gathered for two hours and took turns getting up to speak in front of strangers for progressively longer periods of time. I couldn't tell if it sounded like a fun theater-camp activity or my worst nightmare come true.

A week later, I showed up to the speaking circle right on time. My hands were clammy, my armpits sweaty. The other five people were already there—all my seniors by at least twenty years and all in business attire. I noticed an old video camera set up on a tripod. It seemed like we were about to make an amateur movie rather than some real emotional strides.

We were told we each had to stand up and tell a story about anything, all while being filmed. At the end we'd be sent our video to watch. That sounded simple enough. I could do this. These people were strangers anyway. I had nothing to lose. No reason to be nervous. No reason at all.

But of course when my turn came, all I wanted to do was slowly and quietly back away toward the door, shake my head and whisper "no thank you." I was more than nervous. I was dizzy, my face felt red, and my mouth was parched. But I had to do it. Everyone was waiting. So I started small, by introducing myself. I told them my name, that I had two older brothers, where I went to school, that I was in eleventh grade. And then that thing happened where you lose your voice midsentence and your body forces you to swallow because your throat is so dry. I lost it.

"Sorry, I'm just so nervous right now," I admitted to all those strangers, speaking quickly. "I don't know why I get this way. I know it's irrational and this doesn't matter and none of you are going to judge me." I touched my face with my wet hands. "Oh man, my face feels so hot right now, it's probably really red." Then I stopped and waited for them to laugh or tell me to sit down, that that was enough. But everyone just sat in silence. No one seemed to mind that I was nervous or that I was admitting it. To them, it was all a part of the exercise. I paused, forcing myself to feel okay with the silence. And then I continued, saying that I'd always wanted a dog, but my dad had never let me have one. That I didn't like listening to music on the subway because it made it hard to eavesdrop and watch people, two of my favorite activities. That I liked chocolate ice cream more than vanilla—most of the time. I rambled until my time was up. I felt liberated and exhilarated by the experience. I had made myself vulnerable in front of these strangers, shared raw emotions, and no one had flinched. Next I watched as one woman got up and told us she just needed to be silent, so she stood there in silence staring at us. Then I watched a grown man in a suit stumble over his words and stammer to get a sentence out, obviously as nervous as I was.

The speaking circle was only two hours of my life, but it completely changed my outlook. It felt good to speak up! I imagined letting go of my fear and saying everything on my mind. Now I just had to figure out how to actually do that.

Another important development was happening in my life around this time—my oldest brother began working at a start-up called Teespring. Through Teespring's website and app, people can design and sell T-shirts. If enough people buy a specific shirt, Teespring prints and delivers them. The company was hugely successful and growing rapidly—all thanks to its ingenious business model, which was only possible, as my brother explained to me, because of code. Teespring was also enabling people who had large social-media followings to launch T-shirt campaigns geared toward their fans—this, too, was only possible through code, since social media is built on it. I had no idea what coding actually was, but when my brother talked about it, he made it sound like an all-powerful tool. I wondered whether coding was another form of expression, like writing, that I could use to speak up. Maybe it could even help me achieve my dream of greatness by letting me share my ideas without using my actual voice.

My brother told me that coders were in high demand in the job market; they got paid a lot of money; they got to work at fancy places with free food and Ping-Pong tables; and, most importantly, they made things I loved, things that made a huge impact on the way people connected and shared information, like Google, my beloved Snapchat, and Facebook. Those amazing companies all ran on code. I needed to learn how to do it. Clearly coding meant expression, and it also meant power. The power to build something great. The power to build the next Google or Snapchat or anything I dreamed of.

Unsure what to do from there, I did some research and

found out about Girls Who Code, an organization that ran a summer coding intensive for girls. I applied and, a few months later, found out I was accepted. I was excited, but I still didn't really know what coding was, and I didn't really know if I'd be any good at it. Was it letters or numbers or a mixture of both? Did you do it in a Google doc or did you need a special program to code? Would I have to make flash cards and memorize coding nouns and coding verbs and coding tenses? I hoped not, because I had attempted that with Latin and then with Spanish, and both times I couldn't even make a sentence even after years of classes. But people did call coding a language, so what else could it be? Well, I was about to find out.

A LITTLE BIT ABOUT ANDY

ANDY

I can't remember when I first fell in love with video games, but it was probably back when I thought Lunchables were cool. As soon as my dad (a computer programmer) came home from work, I'd follow him to our family computer and watch him play a bootleg copy of the military sci-fi strategy game *StarCraft*. If I harassed him enough, he'd hand me the controls, and I'd excitedly take over. I'd lose pretty quickly—I was five and had no concept of strategy. But I was ever the optimist, and despite frequent and harrowing losses, playing *StarCraft* with my dad was one of my favorite activities. It took us out of our normal world and transported us to another one entirely.

I didn't just play video games to do that—like any five-year-old, I was obsessed with playing pretend. I would pretend that I had superpowers, or that I was in high school, or that I was solving mysteries like Nancy Drew or Harriet the Spy. In these fantasies I was always older, with the complete freedom to do anything without anyone else's permission. I loved creating and building my own world, and interacting with it—if not literally (with sheets and pillow forts), then in my imagination.

The best part was having sisters who played right alongside me. I had two—my twin sister, Kate, and Gia, two years our senior. Kate, Gia, and I encouraged one another to stretch our imaginations: together we built complex story lines, rearranged pillows and mattresses for our games, chose characters for each other. We played with boys' toys as much as girls' toys, and even though some relatives told us to stick to what girls "should" be doing, we didn't care one bit about gender norms. We gravitated toward Star Wars, Yu-Gi-Oh, and football, as much as horses and dolls. And we loved watching movies on our VHS player. My all-time favorite was *Atlantis: The Lost Empire*. I was obsessed with one of the characters, Audrey. Audrey Ramirez was Hispanic and she was maybe seventeen years old, making her the youngest member of the Atlantis exploration crew. But even more magnificent was her role: mechanical engineer. By the time Audrey joined the team, she was incredibly skilled, talented, and capable of doing her job; her gender, ethnicity, and age didn't matter. I watched the movie over and over because I wanted to be like her. So I sought out other stories about smart, daring girls: Alanna in Tamora Pierce's Lioness Quartet, Corbin Bleu in *Catch That Kid*, Nudge in Maximum Ride, Garth Nix's Abhorsen series, Mulan in *Mulan*—the list of books about "hacker kids" and empowered female protagonists got longer and longer. After spending so much time with Kate and Gia, I was eager to differentiate myself. I needed to find my own identity.

Besides my sisters, I grew up with two other strong female forces. There was my *lola* (grandma), Teresita, who loved to sing and whine about how we weren't eating enough, constantly cooking and baking in an attempt to fix that. And there was my mama, Lorna, a nurse at the New York Eye and Ear Infirmary, down the street from our apartment. We all lived in the East Village in New York City and were enveloped in the thriving Filipino enclave there. Through food, parties, and people, we had a tight-knit community where I celebrated Filipino culture. Although no one was thrilled about the NYU students who lived near us and expanded like a virus, growing up in the East Village made me appreciate being part of a group and creating a shared sense of purpose and love.

My mother had been raised in a small town outside Manila, in the Philippines, and her family never had much money. They constantly worried about making ends meet, so she studied to become a nurse. Back in the eighties, the United States was granting visas to nurses in the Philippines because of a major nurse shortage here. With a nursing degree, my mama could come to the United States, have a stable income, and send money back home. When she got her degree, she wasn't looking for something she was passionate about—she was looking for a way to provide for her family. She doesn't talk to us about her family a lot, but when she does, I'm always blown away by the sacrifices she made to give them a better life. But her sacrifices put a lot of pressure on me to follow what my family thought was best. My dreams felt like they were less about me and more about giving back to the people I cared about.

My parents always wanted the best for us. And to them, the best for us was lots of money. Since my parents didn't have much while growing up in the Philippines, they prioritized financial stability over everything else. They believed economic stability equaled happiness, and my parents drilled that into our heads from a very early age. When we were little, my parents presented us with three paths: doctor, lawyer, or engineer. And to become any of those, we'd have to be good students. So from the beginning, they directed everything we did toward learning—watching television to learn, reading to learn, listening to music to learn. I wasn't allowed to watch *SpongeBob SquarePants* or the Disney Channel. But aside from the fact that I couldn't see *Kim Possible* whenever I wanted, I didn't mind so much—I liked the idea of doing well for myself and for my parents. For elementary school, they enrolled me in the Special Music School, a selective public school (which kids audition for at age four) where I'd get a rigorous conservatory-style piano education along with a traditional academic one. My older sister already went there, and my family thought going to the Special Music School would give me a prestigious learning experience, and my potential piano proficiency would provide me with better opportunities in the future.

As it turned out, I ended up with the best teacher in the entire school—if you could handle her. During my lessons with Genya Paley, she'd yell at me and slam her hands on the piano. I'd cry, pausing from playing only to wipe tears from the keys. It may sound like it was torture . . . but it was boot camp, it was tough love. My school became my family, and my music became my life. And in my Special Music School family, I felt like an equal. At SMS and in music, a girl could be just as musical as a boy—the highest quality of work was expected from *everyone*. And luckily for me, I was pretty damn musical and good at piano. I was just as good as, if not better than, my classmates, and I was judged solely on my abilities as a musician—not my race, gender, or anything else out of my control. Going to SMS shaped how I thought about gender equality and influenced how I felt about myself. It was hard, and I didn't have time for friends or hobbies out of school, but I learned a lot from SMS, inside and outside the classroom.

Fast-forward to the summer after eighth grade: I was still studying piano with Genya, but two years earlier I had decided to put my class notes before my music notes, and I applied (and was accepted!) to Hunter College High School. Life was great, but I was already fourteen. By that age, *Atlantis*'s Audrey Ramirez was already a supervisor at her dad's workshop. I was really behind if I aspired to be like her, and I couldn't afford to lose more time. The thing is, I didn't know anything about how to become an engineer like Audrey. All I knew was that I was going to be one. And basically every engineer has some coding experience, so I tackled that first. Coding also seemed the most accessible: I was old enough to use a computer, I had a computer, and it seemed a lot safer than a fourteen-year-old waving around wrenches and screwdrivers.

So I went to my parents and told them I wanted to learn to program at a coding camp. As was typical, they answered, "If it's cheap and nearby, yes. Where?"

But I didn't know where. This was the first moment in my life I really had control over how I spent time related to my career and future. So I researched, Googled, compared prices—but everything was expensive and inconvenient. The only free program I could find was something called Girls Who Code . . . but I had already missed the application deadline. Plus, it was for high school juniors and seniors and I was only an eighth grader. I guess I would have to wait for that one. In desperation, I nervously emailed an organization in

Westchester called SummerTech Computer Camps, asking if they granted financial aid. I was a pretty shy person—I had never asked anyone for something this big. It was the first time I really put myself out there, and to someone I didn't even know! And besides, I was in eighth grade. . . . Who was going to listen to an eighth grader? I expected I'd have to suck it up and look somewhere else. But the camp director responded and said I could go for a much cheaper rate: still an expensive rate, but one my parents begrudgingly agreed to pay. I was ecstatic, and forwarded him my parents' and my information. A week later, I checked their website to make sure that they had processed everything correctly. They had . . . but they put my name under the "Parents" information and my father's under "Camper." It was incredible—I must have sounded so grown-up they thought I was the parent.

At the start of July, my papa drove me up to Westchester. I marched through the door, signed my name to the attendance book, and entered the room where the rest of the campers were. Then my heart stopped.

They were all boys, huddled around computers and talking to each other, playing video games on their DSs. The room seemed like a totally different universe. Anxiously, I scanned the room for people without a Y chromosome. There were two . . . but they were staff members. I had heard that there weren't a lot of girls in STEM (science, technology, engineering, and mathematics), but I didn't understand how bad it was. *That's why they put my dad's name down as the camper—because he's a guy.* I sat down, a bit regretful about my decision to come here. I felt out of place.

Eventually, we signed up for different classes and split into groups. I was struck with a slew of new fears. What if everyone here already knew how to code? Was this beginner's group really a beginner's group? What if I couldn't keep up? I was already doubting my abilities as a computer programmer before I'd even started. I was surrounded by people who looked different from me, *were* different from me, and it made me feel like I couldn't do it. Like I didn't belong. We stayed in our chairs, and our counselor, Roger, circled our table, setting up our development environments. "Now, in Java, and a lot of other languages, the first thing you need to know how to make is a print statement," he began.

A print statement makes your computer show text on its screen—but back then, I didn't know what printing meant, and I wasn't sure if "statement" meant something different for computer programmers. . . . I was already overwhelmed.

"Now listen to what I say, and type it."

"System,"

System

"dot,"

System.

"out, dot,"

System.out.

"print,"

```
System.out.print
```

"l, n,"

```
System.out.println
```

"open parenthesis, close parenthesis, semicolon."

```
System.out.println();
```

"Now! Inside the parentheses, type 'Hello World' in quotation marks."

```
System.out.println("Hello World");
```

No, that's not right, I thought. Why were we even typing words, anyway? I thought this was going to be 1s and 0s, like they do in the movies. My screen wasn't even black and green . . . wasn't that what it was supposed to look like?

"Now press the green Play button to run your code!"

With a deep breath, I did. On the bottom of the screen, a panel showed up with the words "Hello World" output in small letters.

"You did it! Yaaay!" Roger laughed and walked around, making sure we'd all typed it correctly. "Great! Now you can play around with what you can print out and what you can't, using System-dot-out-dot-print-l-n."

And that was just day one. As the week went on, I gained confidence in my basic programming skills. I became friends with the campers, and told my parents to pick me up later so I could spend more time with them after classes. I registered for four more weeks, spending two of them with Roger and the other two in an advanced class with an instructor named

Sam. The camp director, Steve, lowered my tuition even further, ensuring that I could attend for the rest of the summer. In exchange, I acted as a sort of representative for an idea he had to make a branch of the camp specifically for girls. He hoped to foster a positive environment for young women, so the classes would all be taught by girls, and you'd learn in rooms with all girls, while still being able to have a co-ed camp environment outside the classroom. Steve brought in filmmakers, recorded campers and counselors talking about SummerTech's learning environment, and even soundtracked part of the video with me singing on my ukulele. Later on, a local newspaper came to interview Steve and the campers about the next summer's girls' program, and I excitedly answered their questions.

After that experience, I was excited to make a difference in my community and inspire more girls like myself—those who were ready to learn how to code but weren't sure if they could do it. Plus, I had found a STEM field that I enjoyed and that satisfied my parents' mantra of "doctor, lawyer, engineer"!

So at age twelve, I had decided on my career path: I'd be a programmer and I'd do everything in my power to pursue that goal—coding

would be my "thing." But, then, once I entered high school, I threw myself into other hobbies and activities I enjoyed, too. I continued to devote a lot of time and attention to piano; I joined the volleyball team; I joined the school choir. I became involved in the theater community, working backstage on props and as an assistant stage manager. I spent a lot of time building robots on my robotics team, where I didn't code at all since I was working on hardware. I still loved coding, but I was also developing many other passions as I explored my wider interests and talents.

It began to feel as if the identity I'd made for myself as a computer programmer was cracking. I wondered whether I was committing to a path in computer science too early in life—what if I had convinced myself I liked computer science only because of my parents' influence? As much as I loved all the academic and extracurricular work I did, I hated the intense pressure to succeed: pressure from my parents and pressure from within myself. And, specifically, pressure to succeed in something that would land me a lucrative job out of college rather than what necessarily what made me happiest. I wondered if all that pressure was coloring my choices.

So during my junior year of high school, I applied to Girls Who Code. I hoped that spending seven weeks of my summer in an intensive coding program would help me decide if I should make computer science my college major and career aspiration. I really did love coding, but I wanted to make sure I loved it because it made me happy, not because I knew pursuing it would make my parents happy.

3

GIRLS, GIRLS, GIRLS (WHO CODE)

SOPHIE

On a clammy July morning the summer before my senior year of high school, I arrived at the IAC building in downtown Manhattan wearing a men's Hawaiian shirt, black with red flowers. I figured that wearing such a loud shirt would make people think I was confident and secure—even though I was feeling anything but. It had become my go-to article of clothing to wear on the first day of anything.

I locked my bike down the block and walked slowly to the main entrance of the building, which was stout and angular and made entirely of white glass. It looked like an ice cream cake. I slyly adjusted my outfit, pulling down my skirt and combing my fingers through my windblown hair. It was 8:50. In ten minutes I would begin my first day of the seven-week Girls Who Code summer program.

My heart was beating faster than normal, and the forty-eight-hour deodorant I'd globbed on an hour ago was no help with the nervous sweating. Part of me wished I wasn't here in my loud Hawaiian shirt and was instead at home, sleeping until noon.

I entered the Ice Cream Cake to find a circle of silent girls, eyes darting from the ceiling to one another to the security desk to me. Girls who were shorter than me and girls who were taller than me (not many) and girls with different skin tones than mine and different hair colors and girls whose parents had taken the full hour ride on the subway to get here because they were scared to let their daughters ride it alone and then one girl whose parents had dropped her off in a fancy car on the way to work. I was the only one who had ridden a bike.

I was excited about the diversity in the group. For the first time ever I was going to be a minority: in a class of twenty, there were only four white girls. But while there was racial diversity, there was zero gender diversity. And other than the tennis or soccer team, I had never been part of an all-girls anything before. Something felt vaguely culty about the homogeny. It was strange that we didn't know each other at all, but were now somehow bonded through our gender. Still, I could tell that everyone else felt vaguely uncomfortable to be surrounded by so many strangers.

As I stood there scanning the group, I realized that I had never once imagined a coder as a girl. I'm embarrassed to admit it now, but until that moment, my mental image of a coder was a young guy in a ratty Star Wars T-shirt and sweatpants hunched over a large desktop in the corner of a room, headphones atop a greasy head of hair. I wondered why I had never pictured a girl . . . probably because I'd never seen a female coder before. I'd seen pictures of the founders of Google and Facebook and other major tech companies, but they were all men. I had watched movies and TV shows that depicted hackers, but they had all been men too.

Reshma Saujani created Girls Who Code for that very reason. Not all coders look like the one in my imagination, but most coders, and engineers in general, are male. I was shocked to learn that, according to the National Center for Women & Information Technology, as of 2015, only 25 percent of coders were women. And of that 25 percent, only 5 percent were Asian, only 3 percent were African-American, and only 1 percent were Latina. Which is ridiculous when you consider that 58 percent of all college grads are women. I thought about the apps, products, and forms of entertainment we're missing out on as a society because there are so few women working in tech. If there are more women in tech, and more diversity among the women in the field, there will be many more and different ideas, since females bring a unique point of view to the table. And as more women go into tech, that in and of itself will attract even more women by providing inspiration to young girls. It's hard to imagine yourself doing something if there aren't role models who look like you doing it too.

At nine sharp we were guided upstairs, the twenty of us stuffing into two elevators (bonding!). The IAC building was home to numerous tech companies, including Vimeo, Dictionary.com, Match.com, and Tinder, all owned by the umbrella company IAC. My same older brother who worked at Teespring had told me about the "tech world," a term that seemed to be cooler than "finance" and "consulting" and "being an adult," but still in the same category. He had painted that enticing picture of free food, fancy offices, and lots of Ping-Pong tables, but I just assumed he was exaggerating. But now here I was, actually getting a peek at it firsthand. And as we walked off the elevator and through the kitchen area, I saw his stories were true. The kitchen seemed more like a supermarket, with endless piles of glossy snack bags: potato chips and pita chips, plus their cousins, pretzels and popcorn. Next to those were shelves of candy bars, again of every shape, size, and flavor, and even one of those magic whatever-you-want soda machines.

We finally came to our destination, a large conference room down the hall. Light poured in through the glass walls. As I grabbed a chair up front, I spotted the Empire State Building in the distance, buried behind rows and rows of towering skyscrapers in midtown Manhattan. I couldn't believe this incredible view would be mine for the summer. The tech world seemed to entail unlimited free food, fancy buildings with stunning views, and the people

who made the apps in my phone. My Hawaiian shirt was cool, but this was cooler.

Our teacher, Sean, started off the day by listing all the things that ran on code. I found out it wasn't just Google, Snapchat, and Facebook. Streetlights and airplanes and printers and cash registers and fancy coffee machines also ran on code. "What is this magic?" I said (in my head). "All those things rely on code to function?" I thought about my morning, about the iPhone alarm that had woken me at seven a.m., the microwave I used to heat up last night's lasagna (dinner for breakfast is the way to go), the stoplight that turned red just in time so a Toyota didn't run me over on my way downtown. According to Sean, I wouldn't have been able to get through the past two hours without the wizardry of code. It was everywhere, humming under the surface of everything, and now I was about to learn how to wield its power. If code was essential to almost everything in my daily life, then maybe by learning how to do it, I could fulfill my dream of having an impact on lots of people.

But Sean wasn't done tantalizing us. He pulled up a simple text editor (basically, a blank white window that you can type in) on his computer and projected his laptop screen onto a large canvas at the front of the room. He set a timer for one minute and then typed furiously. Every few lines looked vaguely like English, except with lots of brackets and parentheses and curly braces that look like this: }. I spotted the word "print" multiple times and lots of the phrase "Hello World," and he kept going and going and going, stopping only for brief interludes to remember what to type next.

```
1   Java
2
3   public static void main (String[] args) {
4     System.out.println("Hello World!");
5   }
6
7   C++
8
9   #include <iostream>
10  using namespace std;
11  int main(){
12    cout<<"Hello World!"<<endl;
13  }
14
15  Python
16
17  if _name_ == "_main_":
18    print("Hello World!")
```

Sean's code looked sort of like instructions. And as I would come to learn, code at its simplest really is just a list of instructions that a person writes and a computer reads and carries out. But code has to be incredibly specific, because computers are actually pretty dumb, and they need to be told exactly what to do to get the job done.

Coding is like making a peanut butter and jelly sandwich for someone who has never heard of either ingredient, never opened a jar, or used a knife. You can't just tell them to put jelly and peanut butter on a piece of bread and smush it together. You need to explain how to pick up the bread and how to pull it out of the packaging and then how to open the jar and how to pick up the knife. . . . You need to break down the larger task into every possible tiny, little step. And if your steps don't make sense, you get a coder's worst nightmare: a "bug," the programming term for when a program fails to run the way you expect it to. The bug will either make the computer follow the steps incorrectly (like trying to spread the peanut butter on the plate instead of on the bread), or the program won't run at all. In that case you're usually left with lots of error messages. Think: the PB&J maker shouting in your ear about everything in your instructions that doesn't make sense.

When the sixty seconds were up, Sean pressed Enter and "Hello World" showed up over and over and over again in another window. Sean explained that he had just written a simple Hello World program in several different coding languages, including JavaScript, Python, and Objective-C. Each coding language operates on the same principles, but each has slightly different rules, slightly different syntax, slightly different placements of the brackets, and is built for different tasks. For example, most websites are built using JavaScript, HTML, and CSS, whereas most iPhone apps are built in Swift or Objective-C. Languages have tradeoffs between how easy they are for a programmer to write in and how quickly a computer can process their instructions. Usually, the simpler a language is for a human to write, the harder (and slower) it is for a computer to process. But like the Romance languages that all derive from the same base and have similar but slightly different words and sentence structures, coding languages all follow certain patterns but with slight variations.

So this was coding. You didn't do it in a Google doc. There weren't nouns and verbs like other languages (although I did see a lot of familiar English). I was impressed by Sean's magic and I could tell I wasn't the only one. The girls around the table were smiling, eyes transfixed. We all wanted in. We all wanted our fingers to move like that, to have the power to make a computer respond to our touch. That day we got to create our own Hello World programs. Writing a Hello World program was like learning to say "My name is Sophie" on the first day of Spanish class, letting *"Me llamo* Sophie" fall from your mouth before you learn that the *o* on the end of *"llamo"* indicates the first person. It's a rite of passage. As I coded I felt like I was doing magic, even though I was just copying words into the text editor and pressing Enter. Every time the "Hello World" popped up, I felt a jolt of excitement.

The first few days of Girls Who Code were a blur of learning names, finding a new routine, and gaining some coding basics. Coding was different from anything I could have expected. It wasn't similar to what I had ever done in math or science class. And actually, the only math it required was basic arithmetic. Coding was a new way of thinking, because it required you to think about everything like the clueless PB&J maker. And the better you were at problem solving, the better you were at coding.

Midway through the first week we got our first assignment of the summer: create a virtual slot machine with whatever theme—e.g., sports, a famous person, pop culture—we chose. It sounded like a cool project, but I was nervous. What if I couldn't figure out how to solve it? What if I was terrible at coding? Even worse, I had to work on the project with another girl, Karla, which meant there would be no way for me to struggle silently. I had wanted to learn to code because it seemed like an alternative way to speak up, a way to express my thoughts yet not be put on the spot. But now, if I was confused or wrong or bad at this, someone else would know. There was no room for revision, nowhere to hide. The nerves and anxiety that plagued me whenever I had to speak in class started to bubble up.

That week we were working in Scratch, which MIT developed to teach kids as young as eight the basic concepts of coding. Instead of typing out letters and numbers as part of one set of instructions, like Sean had done with the Hello World programs, Scratch lets you visually build and "snap" together a series of instructions. The instructions look a bit like puzzle pieces and range from "repeat x number of times" to "move forward x steps." The whole Scratch experience feels sort of like a computer game.

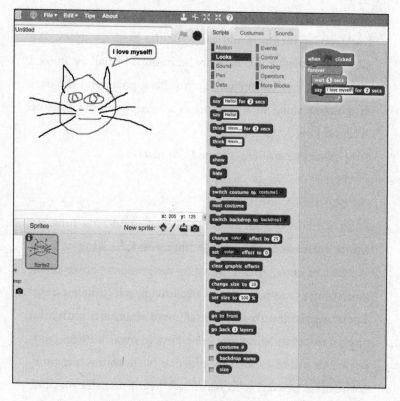

This is what Scratch looks like. The blocks with premade instruction are provided in the center. The user drags them to the space on the right, and the "canvas," where things actually happen, is on the left. The program shown here makes the cat say "I love myself!" every five seconds.

"So let's build a slot machine!" I said, trying to break the silence. Karla gave me a "Yes, but how?" smile. I felt myself relax a little. At least she seemed to be as clueless about how to start as I was.

"What should our slot machine's theme be?" she asked. Karla was evidently ready to tackle the hard questions. We sat in more silence. I racked my brain until I finally stumbled upon a series of old memories: my Elvis phase and the days of dancing alone in my room as a seven-year-old blasting "Hound Dog."

"Let's make an Elvis-themed slot machine."

"Elvis?"

"Elvis!"

So Karla and I sat in more silence pondering how we would go about mashing up gambling and the King of Rock 'n' Roll in code. And how were we going to break down something as complex as a slot machine into its simplest steps? These instructions would be far more elaborate, with a lot more steps, than telling someone how to make a PB&J sandwich. We had to explain to someone (well, to the computer, not really a person) who had never heard of a slot machine how a slot machine worked and how to use it. Sean had given us some instructions, but I didn't know where to begin. I had never built anything with code before; I hadn't even known what coding was a few days before. But time was passing. We had to just start somewhere. "Let's try to write out the most general steps that a real-life slot machine would follow and then go from there," I suggested. Part of what makes coding so cool and creative is that there are countless ways to go about coding any problem, just as there are countless ways to explain making a peanut butter and jelly sandwich. And just as more complex dishes require more complex recipes, more complex tasks require more complex code. It's the coder's job to decide how to go about solving the puzzle, and the best coders are able to identify and execute the simplest solutions to the most complex problems.

These are the basic steps we came up with:

1. If the user presses the slot machine's Spin button, then the machine should spin all three reels.

2. The machine should randomly choose one image on each reel to stop at.

3. If all three reels have the same image, then the user wins.

What had seemed so overwhelming, what had brought us to uncomfortable silence only minutes before, now seemed much more doable. We continued to break down each step into smaller and smaller steps, turning our English words into code when the steps became simple enough for the computer to understand. Scratch made it easy to implement a lot of our instructions because it came with already-coded functions and tools. For instance, it was easy for us to tell the computer when to "hide" images (i.e., before the user presses

Spin) and when to "show" images (i.e., after the reels stop spinning). Scratch also made adding buttons super easy by allowing us to draw rectangles and tell the computer to do a set of instructions when we clicked them.

We found photos of Elvis on Google Images and placed different ones in three general areas on the Scratch screen. Imagine dragging a bunch of photos into a Word document and putting some overlaid on top of each other on the left of the page, some in the middle, and some on the right. We wrote the code so that all the photos started out in a hidden state, which meant that while they were technically on the screen, the user couldn't see them. Then we told the computer that when the user pressed the Spin button, it should choose one of the images in each pile at random and change its state from "hidden" to "show," so it became visible to the user. This way we tricked the user into thinking that three images popped up randomly, when really they were all there the whole time. We also downloaded a track of "Hound Dog" and told the computer to play it when the user pressed the Spin button.

A few hours later we sat staring at our creation. It was a beauty. The slot machine included different pictures of the man himself, Mr. Presley, and the computer cooed "Hound Dog." We high-fived and laughed, proud of what we'd made. Karla and I had built a whole virtual slot machine where there was only a blank screen hours before. I had experienced firsthand the force of code to create something from nothing, and it made me feel powerful. The sense of accomplishment completely eclipsed all the anxiety I'd had about working with another person. Actually, working with Karla had been positive. We'd figured it out together, filling in each other's gaps when one of us was confused.

That day, when each team presented their slot machine to the class, I was amazed at all the funny, cool themes other groups had chosen. One in particular stood out. It was a rap-themed slot machine with Biggie's, Tupac's, and Lil Wayne's faces flanking the virtual reels. One of its creators got up to present it. I noticed her green Doc Martens, her Warby Parker–esque glasses, and her music taste (made clear by the theme of her slot machine). I took note—this girl seemed cool. She even had a cool name, Andy. Maybe we'd be friends?

Every few days we got a new challenge to tackle, as well as a new randomly assigned partner. At first, each assignment brought a fresh wave of anxiety, even though my first experience with Karla had been so positive. I felt forced to prove my intelligence and coding skills to yet another classmate every time. Each pair would chug along at one computer, taking turns on the keyboard, so there really was no hiding if I didn't know how to solve a problem or if I was confused. We'd break down larger tasks into small, codable bits just as we had done with the slot machine challenge, and then talk through how to do each step together.

Even though the collaborating made me feel anxious, I loved those weeks coding in that beautiful room in the Ice Cream Cake. We laughed and coded, and we talked and coded, and some of us even cried and coded.

Okay, tears over code actually only happened once, and they were tears of joy. Joy that was so intense because the frustration leading up to it had been equally intense. The group assignment that day was to use JavaScript to make rectangles of different heights that randomly generated and scrolled across the screen when someone ran the program. It hadn't seemed that hard as I read over the assignment in the morning, but when I sat down with my partner to map out how we would tackle the project, I was intimidated by the idea of starting, just like with the slot machine. I wondered where to even begin. I nervously hoped she was feeling the same way so I wouldn't be the dud of the team.

Coding is similar to constructing a building in that you need a blueprint first. But it felt like I didn't even know how to draw a line on the page. This assignment was the hardest one yet. The first step was to figure out how we would make so many different rectangles show up, each one with its own height. If we were going to make a new rectangle with a new height every second, then we had to find a general and efficient way to do that. But how? I kept zoning out as I looked out the window at the Empire State Building. This "tech" thing didn't seem as fun anymore. My brother had been right about the free food and fancy offices, but he hadn't explained that sometimes it's difficult and frustrating work.

That day, polygons were the largest issue in my life, and I could tell that I wasn't the only one struggling.

Around the table sat ten pairs of girls with twenty small pink computers propped open in front of them, talking or spacing out in thought over the assignment. We were all stumped. Then, slowly, different pairs had their own *aha* moments, and it was exciting to watch the glee as each group discovered the answer. Finally it clicked for me too.

I turned to my partner, Emma, and exclaimed, "We need to use classes!"

Classes were a new concept that week. Programmers use classes to generalize objects with the same traits but different values. For example, "Car" might be a class. All Cars have wheels and a frame (i.e., the same traits), but different types of Cars, from trucks to station wagons, have different numbers of wheels and different-sized frames (i.e., different values). In our case, we would make a class called "Rectangles." All Rectangles have heights (in the same way all Cars have wheels), but we wanted each new rectangle to have a height of a different value (e.g., some with a height of fifty pixels and some with a height of seventy pixels). We could make a new Rectangle "object" every second, and each object could have a different height. Then we could tell all the Rectangle objects to move across the screen. We smiled and high-fived, and maybe I stood up and did a little dance Elvis-style, and then we got to work actually coding our project.

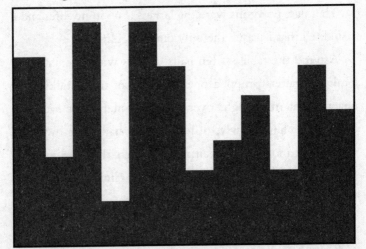

We stopped being joyful quickly. It gave us some comfort to know that, again, we weren't alone; all the other teams were frustrated too. Some girls held their heads in their hands, some shouted out "It's not working," some laughed, some ate their feelings in the form of an early lunch, and I slumped down in my chair and let my legs go limp. By midday the beautiful glass room, made for high-class businesspeople to drink coffee together and show each other flow charts and bar graphs, was a zoo of angry teenage girls, causing Sean and our frantic TAs to run around trying to quell the animals. I don't think anyone in that room had ever hated rectangles so much.

But little by little, each pair got their rectangles scrolling and each pair got their own applause from the rest of the group. And then those tears of joy finally flowed as soon as that one classmate made her program work. My partner and I were among the last groups to finish, but I didn't feel bad or dumb or judged that day. Watching how supportive everyone was helped me see that no one cared how long it was taking us to get it. They would just be proud of us when we did.

As I rode my bike home that afternoon, I felt thoroughly triumphant. Watching my rectangles scroll across the screen had eclipsed all the frustration and head-banging from earlier that day. All I could think about was what I had created. I again felt powerful. If I could make rectangles scroll, then what else could I do? The possibilities seemed limitless.

The supportive and collaborative environment at Girls Who Code not only made the projects more enjoyable but also completely changed the way I acted in "class." While I had rarely raised my hand at school, I began to let it go up at Girls Who Code after Sean asked a question and the room fell silent. I would deliberate for a long time in the quiet. Should I do it? Yes. No. Yes. No. And then I would raise my hand, and my heart would beat quickly, but it was a beat of exciting-scary, not actually-shit-yourself-scary like I was used to at school. It didn't seem to matter anymore if I was wrong, if what I had to say was stupid. I knew everyone around the table wanted me to succeed. I had started the summer apprehensive about the all-girls environment, but I discovered that part of the reason I was so comfortable here was precisely because we were all girls. I had never felt uncomfortable learning with guys, but I felt extra safe with all the female students. It's like we were bonded by our common experience, and that made me comfortable enough to take risks and let go of my fear of getting the answer wrong. My few hand raises a day were a step in the right direction, and I was proud of myself for taking those first baby steps outside my comfort zone.

ADULTS ARE COOL TOO!

ANDY

During the first five weeks at Girls Who Code, we spent our time working on small one- or two-day projects. During week one, we trained ourselves to think like coders using Scratch and the slot machines. By the end of week five, we had moved on from Scratch to more advanced languages like JavaScript and Python, making websites and mobile apps. We no longer felt uncomfortable with the prospect of coding—as a group, we launched into our daily projects without fear, knowing that even if we didn't have the answers, we had Sean and one another for support.

As it turned out, I had come into Girls Who Code with a

unique perspective: I already had a solid programming foundation. Only one other girl had programmed before, while everyone else had never come close to writing a line of code. I was able to dive into whatever project we had as soon as Sean presented it and, in many cases, I would finish my own version of the project by the time he was done fielding questions from the class. But all of our projects were done in pairs or trios—so I would start from scratch once I joined up with my partner. Girls Who Code became a whole other type of learning experience for me: explaining concepts to someone without just handing over the code I'd written was a challenge in itself. I wanted my partner to succeed, to feel that sense of success I felt whenever I wrote good code. Giving her the program I'd already made wouldn't do that. So, instead, I learned how to teach: communicating with my classmates, articulating coding concepts without typing them, and reading other people's code—skills I never fully developed before Girls Who Code.

In addition to getting coding lessons and projects, we were each paired with a mentor, a woman who worked at one of the IAC companies, whom we met with once a week. The first time we met our mentors, I wasn't sure what to expect. I never really had a mentor before. What kind of conversations would we have? What would be appropriate to ask her, or tell her? My mind drifted to my favorite teacher-student relationships in pop culture: Qui-Gon Jinn to Obi-Wan Kenobi,

Obi-Wan Kenobi to Anakin Skywalker, Obi-Wan Kenobi to Luke Skywalker. I realized all of these pairs were men. I was excited to have my very own female mentor, someone I could talk to, someone who had gone through the same experiences I would potentially go through.

She turned out to be Nikki Wiles from Vimeo, a site where people can upload their videos to share, either publicly or privately, with others via password-protected web pages. When we first sat down together in her office, it felt a little awkward to have an hour of one-on-one time with a stranger. Girls Who Code had thrown us together and was like, "Now be friends!" Since we didn't know each other, would she really be able to give me meaningful insights on my career?

Nikki Wiles, my mentor at Girls Who Code

Once Nikki started talking about her background, I loved hearing about her career trajectory and found it fascinating how different it was from how I'd envisioned mine. At my age, she still hadn't known what she was going to do when she grew up. It wasn't until she went to college that she found her passion for computer science. After jumping from programming job to programming job, she found herself at Vimeo . . . but not as a programmer. As a senior technical project manager, Nikki manages teams of people, typically on the technical side of things, to create features that Vimeo uses to run its site ("the back end"), or features visible on the site that users interact with ("the front end"). One week, Nikki invited me to sit in on a design meeting with her coworkers. As I watched her work, it was clear that her education as a computer scientist and her experience as a programmer allowed her to easily straddle the dual world of programmers and designers. Programmers posed problems or obstacles they had while developing, and she understood, reinterpreting technical things to nontechnical people on her team. Her job wasn't coding; it was leading. She actively, excitedly, and easily communicated with team members, monitored their progress, and made sure their projects were executed well. While she never coded during her job, she used her knowledge of computer science to get a better grasp on what her technical team members got done or needed to get done.

Week after week, I gained so many valuable insights and experiences from Nikki. I looked forward to our Tuesday meetings, and I frequently sought her advice. I asked a lot of her, from things as small as stickers from her office to stuff as big as life advice about computer science and my career. She always delivered, helping me understand myself and the possibilities ahead of me. Through our conversations, I saw more and more that computer science isn't a stand-alone field of study—CS bleeds into every aspect of life, and I discovered that I could apply CS to music, English, and social justice, in the same way that Nikki applied CS to her passion for leadership, communication, and management.

For such a long time, I had conditioned myself to think that learning to code and getting a degree in CS meant I was going to be a programmer for the rest of my life. But as I watched Nikki in action, I understood that even if I studied computer science in college, I could still apply those skills to pursue something else if I didn't want to work as a coder. I loved coding, there was no doubt about it—but I felt like maybe I had been too single-minded in my direction. What if I realized I hated coding down the line? If I wasn't going to become a programmer, what else would I be able to do? Either way, I always thought my college degree would define my future and the opportunities available to me. Nikki's life story refuted that.

But as exciting as that realization was, I worried my parents would think I would have less direction and become derailed from the career that I had planned for myself. Gia, my older sister, fought very hard to major in English, and my parents were worried (and still worry) about her financial stability. So I decided my family didn't have to know. At least not for now.

SOPHIE

As the weeks passed at GWC, I was discovering that I had a voice and wanted to use it during our coding classes, and

I was also learning little by little to believe in myself, partly thanks to the many speakers who came to talk to us throughout the summer.

Laura Arrillaga-Andreessen, more than anyone else that summer, embodied for me the can-do spirit that Girls Who Code was fostering in us. Laura challenged me to think about myself in a way that no one had before, in a way that still resonates with me now. And she was definitely practicing what she preached. Laura is a national leader in philanthropy, working hard to create social change and transform our world. She is a founder and president of the Laura Arrillaga-Andreessen Foundation, an organization that educates and inspires philanthropists to make their giving have greater impact and meaning.

When Laura walked through the door, with her chic all-black outfit and loud voice, she immediately caught our attention. It was clear by her energy alone that she was a big personality. She told us to find our passion and not just pursue it, but live it. She clearly was doing that.

"Everyone think about your superpower," she started off by instructing us.

We sat in silence, thinking. Then Laura pointed at one of the girls around the table, Kiana, and asked her to stand up with her feet spread wide, her chin up, and her hands on her hips. Kiana did so with hesitance, obviously slightly uncomfortable for being singled out and having everyone watch her stand in this unnatural pose.

"Now say your superpower."

Laura cold-called girl after girl. Each one stood up and named her superpower, from being good at math to being a good collaborator. Laura offered words of encouragement in response and also suggestions about how each girl could improve her posture, put her shoulders back, stand solidly on two feet, lift her chin, raise her arms, and strengthen her voice. I noticed something incredible: my Girls Who Code friends actually projected greater confidence and power when they followed Laura's recommendations.

I wanted to feel confident and superpowerful like them. But what was my superpower? I sat there thinking in distress, unable to come up with something, hoping I wouldn't get called on. I wasn't good at public speaking, I had no confidence, and I couldn't spell. What was I good at? Playing tennis? I was a mediocre tennis player on a bad high school tennis team. That wouldn't work. Photography? I had taken classes a few summers ago, loved to document my life and spend time in the darkroom. My photos were good enough, but not superpower good. That wouldn't work either. I was good at school. Or at least, I got good grades, but I felt like that was a lame superpower because it didn't really reflect anything about my intelligence.

"Does anyone wish to volunteer?" Laura said after a slew of cold calls. There was dead quiet in the room as we looked around nervously.

In the long silence I came up with a maybe-possibly-I-don't-even-know-if-I-really-believe-it superpower. My grades might not prove that I'm smart, but they did show that when I make goals for myself, I meet them. And when I decided I wanted to learn to code, I met that goal too. I even met smaller goals every day, like riding my bike to Girls Who Code. I realized that once I decide to do something, I don't stop until I achieve it.

"Do it," an internal voice pushed. But I couldn't. I didn't want to have to get up in front of the class and do something so strange as putting my hands on my hips and lifting my chin and saying something positive about myself. In fact, until that moment I couldn't even identify, let alone own, my positive traits. This woman had inspired me. She had told us to find a passion and not just pursue it, but live it. She had told us that we were each future leaders, that she believed in all of us to do good for the world, that we could all make our dreams a reality through our actions. And she had said it all in practically a shout, with an energy that had moved me. An energy that was moving my hand up and into the air and making my mouth open to say, "I'll do it."

Wait! What am I doing?! But there was no turning back.

"Great!" she said as she eyed me, encouraging me to stand up.

And now I was standing, with forty-eight eyes glued to me. I said, "My superpower is that when I set a goal for myself, I do whatever it takes to achieve it, even when it feels like an impossible challenge at first."

"Thanks," she said. "That's so important. We should always embrace a challenge. In fact, self-impose it. Without pushing our limits, we never evolve. Make it matter that you were here."

I sat back down. I had said my superpower out loud, and this real-life superwoman had affirmed it. While I still didn't fully believe I had a superpower, I knew that I really did work hard to reach the goals I set and was proud of myself for having that determination and drive. It occurred to me then and there that I had never considered myself in terms of my positive qualities. I had only ever seen the negative, which meant I always assumed the worst about myself. I assumed I was probably stupid. I assumed I wouldn't actually ever be great, even though I aspired to be. I assumed I would fail. And those fears often held me back from trying new and uncomfortable challenges and experiences and from speaking up. I was so afraid of being judged by everyone else, but really I was the one most judgmental of myself.

So maybe none of my assumptions were right. Maybe I did have something to offer. Laura left us with one final powerful thought: "Be the person you never dreamed it was possible to be." Before she came to speak to us, I couldn't dream in concrete terms of being someone who achieved greatness, or who could help transform other people's lives for the better. But after she left, that was all I could think about. Maybe I did have the power to make a real impact on the world.

5

FINDING THE "ME" IN FEMINISM(E)

ANDY

After five weeks, equipped with new coding skills and insight from intelligent, powerful people from all over the tech industry, we were thrust into our greatest challenge yet: coming up with a final project and executing it through code. I knew I wanted to make a video game, one that would focus on the hypersexualization of women in video games.

As I grew up, I had matured from peering over my dad's shoulder watching him play *StarCraft* to playing video games with my cousins. One of our favorite games was *Tekken*, a popular fighting game. My cousins and I would power through round after round, each choosing a fighter to battle each other with. I always wanted to pick a girl—I'm a girl, and I enjoyed feeling like I was in the game myself, kicking and punching and dodging (and winning). But none of the characters looked like me. I mean, obviously they didn't— I was just a kid at the time—but I knew I would never resemble any of the busty, big-eyed, long-legged women on-screen. Game after game I'd see women who didn't look like me, didn't speak like me, didn't move like me—or any other girl that I knew. All these women looked like Barbie dolls, with big breasts, small waists, and wide hips. I dreamed of making video games with better female characters. But until I learned to code, I didn't have the right tools.

Our household was relatively conservative; when my parents came from the Philippines in the eighties, they brought the gender roles and values of the fifties with them. I was always told to close my legs, hide my bra strap, laugh with my mouth closed. It was unseemly that I had a lot of guy friends, and unthinkable to visit one of their houses alone. My mama often called me out for not looking "like a lady," walking "like a lady." I was used to being uncomfortable with my "lady" self on a day-to-day basis—and seeing the Barbie women on-screen didn't help.

Finally, when my tenth-grade English class read *The Odyssey*, by ancient Greek poet Homer, I had already spent two summers at SummerTech and knew how to code, so I seized the opportunity to design a game from scratch as my final project and address an issue related to the way women are portrayed. (By the way, if you, precious reader, don't know what *The Odyssey* is, I highly suggest attempting a read. It's pretty difficult, but also one of the most important books in the Western canon. You'll feel very worldly and awesome. But, now, back to the video game!)

First I had to figure out what kind of game I was going to make. There are a lot of different types: first-person shooter, role-playing games, platformer, simulation, strategy.

Then it hit me: I would make a side-scroller. With a side-scroller you view the character from a single angle, as if you're an audience member watching a character run across a stage. But the stage goes on for as long as the level is designed, and the character keeps running across the stage, in the same direction. A side-scroller was perfect: it was a nod to retro games like *Super Mario Bros.*, and it would also allow me to create a playable protagonist with villains to fight.

I knew who my protagonist would be: the main character/hunk, Odysseus, as he journeys home from Troy. Through his story, I wanted to explore females' sexual agency in the book. I had a lot to say about Homer's treatment of the female characters, especially in comparison to the treatment of the male characters. Maybe it was my inner feminist, finally feeling brave enough to speak out—Homer's sexism certainly made it easy. New York City is pretty liberal, and I'd go so far as to say Hunter College High School is even more radically left, and I had long been informed about sexism and inequality—but this English project was the first time I took a public stand against it. I was frustrated that Homer portrayed most of the female characters—Calypso, Circe, Nausicaa, Clytemnestra—as villains, not just because they kept Odysseus from getting back to Ithaca, but because they slept with men. In contrast, Odysseus, who cheated on his wife and slept with multiple women, was portrayed by Homer as a hero deserving of the praise and glory the Greek gods and goddesses blessed him with. I cried foul—how was this fair?

It seemed absurd that women were flamed for acting "slutty," while Odysseus could sleep with as many women as he desired without becoming less of a hero. Obviously, I didn't agree with Homer's portrayal of the women in comparison to the men. My solution: a satirical game in which the player would be Odysseus and would have to sweet-talk his way through a bunch of women. Literally *through*—if you pressed a button, a speech bubble saying "Hey <3" would pop out and hit the women, making them disappear. I wanted to overdramatize the ridiculousness of Odysseus's interactions with women to point out how disgustingly womanizing he was.

Given the short time for the project, I set out to make a simple, thirty-second side-scrolling platformer game. In a platformer game, the player guides the main character over a series of suspended platforms or obstacles (think *Super Mario Bros.*). But my "simple" platformer game proved to be much more ambitious than I expected. Unfortunately, I didn't realize this until I started working on the project mere days before it was due. I ended up making the game in four days . . . and two all-nighters, working in my living room, watching coding tutorials on my laptop, and pushing through waves of exhaustion.

Bedraggled and droopy-eyed, I presented my project to the class. I was super nervous—for all I knew, the code wouldn't run, or the whole project would crash and burn. Or, worse, what if no one understood the point of my game? Or maybe people would be upset that I was attacking *The Odyssey* from a modern, feminist angle. Social mores were different in Homer's time, so who was I to say that he had done anything wrong?

When the screen flickered and a window opened,

blinking *THE ODYSSEY: THE GAME*, I took a deep breath and began my presentation. To my surprise, the class burst into laughter as I played the game. I could even hear my English teacher, normally stoic and curt, howling behind me. By the end, my anxiety had completely subsided and I was giggling along with everyone else—frankly, I was excited my code ran at all, but I would never have expected the class to have such a positive reaction to the game. Not only did they understand what I was trying to say, but they liked it. And although it was one of the most exhausting experiences I'd had at that point in my life, it was also one of the most fun—and the most rewarding.

What made the game most effective was how it broke down a complex idea into something accessible and entertaining. There was humor and satire, but it was clear that my game had something to tell you. It was the first time I recognized the potential of using video games as a way to meaningfully engage an audience. I couldn't wait to use this platform again to finally highlight something I cared about deeply: the hypersexualizing of women in video games. So when I learned we would be creating our own projects in the last week at Girls Who Code, I was determined to make that the topic of my final project.

SOPHIE

Unlike Andy, I didn't have a clear vision of what my final project would be, but I did know what I wanted to accomplish with it: the project had to be something that stretched me creatively. The smaller assignments throughout the summer had shown me how incredibly creative coding was. Not only were there many different ways to approach every challenge, I also had the power to bring to life whatever funny or zany idea I had, and in any number of forms. I could make a game or an app or a website. I could use my creativity to decide how the user would interact with my product and what it would look like. I always had random ideas popping into my head, and through the years I had discovered ways to bring them to life: writing stories, taking photographs, making short films, creating Snapchat stories with my friends. Now coding was another one of my creative outlets.

But I wanted to go beyond creativity for this project. I also wanted to do some good for the world. Building something cool and funny would be both cool and funny, but what was the point of making something just for the hell of it? Especially considering I had set out to learn to code as a way of making myself heard. Over the course of the summer I had learned what an incredible tool coding could be for speaking up and creating social change. It felt like my life would only have meaning and purpose if my work did something to help others. Apps, games, and websites (which all run on code) have the ability to reach millions of people globally in a single second. I dreamed of harnessing that power to reach people and change them in a positive way.

Before the summer, the idea of creating a final project would have scared me. It would have seemed overwhelming to come up with a "good" idea and overwhelming to execute it. But Girls Who Code had become a place where I felt safe, comfortable, and supported, so I gave myself permission to pursue whatever weird ideas I came up with. It was so liberating not to feel limited by my fear of judgment, so liberating to know that any unconventional concept would not be shot down as weird or stupid or bad. Alongside these feelings of supportiveness and female bonding—and perhaps because of them—during the course I had also become increasingly interested in issues around women and girls. Feminism, a term I was still figuring out and a term whose meaning in my life I was still deciding, was on my mind a lot by the end of the summer. Before Girls Who Code, I didn't identify as a feminist. I saw feminism as a movement to give equal political and social rights for all genders, and I believed in that. But even though I agreed with everything feminism stood for, I was scared to call myself a feminist. As ridiculous as it seems now, I pictured a feminist as a woman who loved talking about gender equality, but who also liked playing into gender norms that were personally beneficial, like when a guy gave up his subway seat for her or paid for dinner. I didn't want others to assume I was that type of person by calling myself a feminist. It was a point of contention with my close friends during junior year because they were becoming deeply interested in feminism and were involved in the Feminist Club at school. They were annoyed that I believed in everything feminism stood for, and yet wouldn't identify as a feminist.

Then Girls Who Code happened and my feelings about being a feminist, and my understanding of what it meant to me to be a feminist, changed. I began to understand what true girl power was; it's the way that we all supported and encouraged one another, and it's how incredible every girl in the room was. I realized a few weeks into the program that I wanted to identify as a feminist and wanted to do so proudly. All of these girls were so amazing and had so much to offer. I wished all of them, and every other girl, could have the same opportunities and the same support system that our society gives men. Thinking about gender inequality made me feel angry and passionate, inspired me to speak out about it. And

I decided that identifying as a feminist and being the feminist I aspired to be was more important than being scared of what others would see me as when I identified as one.

So here's what I knew: I would build a final project that was creative, that helped people, and that somehow involved feminism. But when the day came to pitch an idea to the wider group and find a partner, I had nothing. So, instead, I hoped one of the other girls would have an idea I could contribute to and collaborate on. But as girl after girl got up and pitched ideas, I wasn't feeling any of them. Everyone had something cool they planned to make, but none of them fit my three criteria. None of them fit me.

Then Andy stood up. Since first taking note of her the day we presented our slot machines, I had spent most lunch breaks with Andy. Even though we came from very different backgrounds, we both went to public high schools in Manhattan, we had a few mutual friends, and we both liked having conversations about larger issues in the world. For whatever reason, we'd never shared our final project ideas with each other, so I was excited to hear her pitch. Andy opened with: "I want to make a game with an activist message—ideally about the hypersexualization of women in video games, but I'd be open to brainstorming new ideas."

WHHAAAAAT. I almost jumped up and down with excitement. I wasn't totally sold on creating a game about the hypersexualization of women in video games, simply because it wasn't a topic I had a personal passion for or connection with (my Neopets obsession was the closest I'd come to being a video game buff). But Andy was clearly interested in pursuing some sort of gender-related issue and had indicated she was open to doing something other than the hypersexualization of women in gaming. Working with her offered the possibility of creating social impact, because we could give the game some sort of message or theme. And there was lots of room for creativity: What would the specific concept and theme be? What would the game look like? How would you play? It was a match made in Girls Who Code final project heaven. I beelined toward Andy, practically pushing people out of the way. I had a really, really good feeling about this.

6

BLOODY FUN

ANDY

When I first arrived at GWC, Sophie caught my eye with her neat sneakers, cool thrifted clothing, and daily bike ride to and from IAC. I wanted to bike to the IAC building too, but my parents never approved the fifteen-mile ride from the Bronx. (My family and I had moved uptown a few years prior.) During lunch breaks when we sat with each other, she'd typically open the conversation by remarking that I got the same sandwich and root beer as yesterday, and I'd confirm, cautiously eyeing her farro or quinoa, grains I'd never seen before meeting Sophie. We talked about a lot of things: music, Bard, Hunter, and sometimes we'd sit with Sean and

discuss pressing social issues. By the time Sophie offered to
partner with me, I was familiar with both farro and quinoa,
and she and I had become pretty good friends.

While I was relieved I'd found a partner to work with, and
as happy as I was it was Sophie, I was ambivalent about having to work with someone else. At SummerTech we didn't
have to collaborate at all. We kept to ourselves with our programming endeavors. Other than talking to my instructor, I
worked alone. I had to account for myself, and no one else.
I didn't really like doing it any other way. I didn't have to
consult anybody about decisions I made, and I had total lib-
erty to do as I pleased. During the first five weeks at Girls
Who Code, I'd had to adjust to working on projects with a
partner, but I didn't find that terribly invasive. You'd work
with one person for one, maybe two, days. But working with
Sophie on our final project . . . that would be a commitment.
If she rejected the ideas I had, I couldn't just stop being her
partner the next day. We had to collaborate on a totally original project, one with no guidelines from Sean, no clear end
product. We'd sink or swim together.

But even more than that, I was afraid of Sophie seeing me
struggle, and working with someone else on an ambitious,
seven-day-long project made me vulnerable to that kind of
scrutiny. I'm the sort of person who believes that if I stare at
a problem long enough, I'll figure out the answer. Which is
absolutely not true. But I had (and still have, to some extent)

issues asking people for help. Asking for help made me feel inadequate, incapable—dumb, even.

And working with someone seven hours a day, for seven straight days? That sounded intensely uncomfortable and near impossible, regardless of how awesome Sophie was.

Immediately after we paired up, Sean encouraged us to get to work—after all, we only had a week to do the project. I nodded to Sophie, and we sat down together at the table. "So . . ." I laughed nervously. Sophie laughed too. "Let's do this."

"I liked the idea of using a game to promote a social message, but I'd like to explore possible issues beyond the hypersexualization of women in video games, if that's okay," Sophie said.

"Absolutely." I was ecstatic that someone had signed on to do this project with me at all, and although I was sad to be scrapping my original idea, I was open to addressing different societal issues.

"So . . . what kind of game are we making?" Sophie said.

"Catcalling?"

"Slut shaming?"

Sophie laughed. I frowned. Nothing was funny about slut shaming, so why was she laughing?

"We should make a game where you throw tampons!" She giggled.

I burst into laughter. It would be really funny if we could

do that, but there was something about it that made me uncomfortable. But I was uncomfortable that I was uncomfortable with making a game involving periods. Gore due to violence is accepted as normal by society, but when it comes to menstrual blood, everybody thinks it's gross. For some reason most people find natural bleeding repulsive. I knew both of these as separate facts, but I didn't put two and two together until that day.

We launched into a discussion about our experiences with this "menstrual taboo." Neither of us had fully understood until that moment the extent to which we'd been conditioned to feel ashamed of our periods.

I talked about watching tampons fall out of a girl's bag in my math class, and how embarrassed that made me feel. Sophie talked about making her mom buy her tampons because she was too embarrassed to buy them herself. I talked about how I tucked tampons up my sleeve whenever I walked down the hallway to a bathroom. She talked about how her guy friends got grossed out when she and her friends mentioned their periods, and I talked about when I was in middle school and everyone panicked over an unwrapped, unused tampon lying in the hallway. The more we shared our menstruation stories and feelings, the more we both recognized the taboo was a major issue.

We also discussed how the way menstrual-product companies market tampons and sanitary napkins reinforces the problem. They employ the vaguest, most nuanced tactics, barely referencing their products at all in their advertisements. Instead they show a woman doing yoga or jumping off a diving board. And if they demonstrate how absorbent the product is, they use a blue liquid, never a red liquid, because suggesting blood would obviously be too gross.

When we Googled "menstrual taboo," we discovered that it's a much more serious problem than just embarrassment about our periods. In the United States, many homeless shelters and women's prisons barely supply tampons or pads for women. Instead they have to find other, often unsanitary, alternatives, even going so far as to reuse pads. In developing countries, girls have it much worse. According to the *Guardian*, 23 percent of girls in India drop out of school when they reach puberty. Often it's because they are too ashamed to take care of their period while in school or don't have the resources. In some small towns in Nepal, women are forced to live in dirty and dangerous shacks while they menstruate because they are considered unclean. We had no idea that the taboo we had experienced was so widespread in our own country as well as part of a much more serious global problem.

"THIS IS CRAZY!" we exclaimed, clicking on Web page after Web page. We became convinced we should do a video game about menstruation to bring the issue to other people's attention and get them talking about it. But how would we persuade Sean and the TAs that our concept—a girl throwing tampons at oncoming enemies—was a totally legitimate project? Sophie, ever the pragmatist, was panicking as she tried to figure out how to pitch our idea to him. And I was panicking because I had never done something this weird before. Which only proved that I had fallen victim to the menstrual taboo myself. Our argument to make the game was solid. There was no reason for me to feel uncomfortable sharing our ideas with Sean . . . and yet, I was.

Sophie and I sat down with Sean, both of us nervous to dive in. His face was friendly and attentive, totally unsuspecting of the bomb we were about to drop.

"Um—" I began. "You remember we're, um, making a video game? Social justice?" *Oh, great effing start, Andy. Good job.*

I trailed off, and my mouth opened and closed, hopelessly searching for words. Sophie stepped in. "We've been brainstorming for the past two hours, trying to figure out messages or ideas we could address with a game, and we came up with something that we thought was worth running by you." Sophie paused. "It's a game where you throw tampons at people. To address the stigma around menstruation."

Sophie and I stumbled our way through the rest of our first presentation together. It was a mess. Think of connect-the-dots—we remembered points we needed to make, made them, and it was up to Sean to see the big picture. Sophie and I talked about our embarrassment about our periods, and how menstrual blood is considered repulsive. We contrasted it with blood from violent games and movies that people are conditioned to be okay with. We talked about how a game about tampons could incorporate humor and satire, and we wanted to get the okay from him before we got going.

Sean stopped to think. "I see what you're saying . . . and I totally agree. I just don't feel comfortable fully green-lighting this until I run it by Reshma and the other higher-ups at GWC."

Sophie and I left with a bittersweet feeling. Sean had taken our idea seriously, but hadn't given us the go-ahead. And, frankly, his response about needing to get approval only validated the menstrual taboo—if we had pitched him a different video game concept, Sean probably would have green-lighted us without blinking an eye.

His reaction made it clear to me and Sophie that our idea was a good one, and that the menstrual taboo was an important social issue we could effectively address through a video game. When we left Girls Who Code that day, we both hoped that Reshma would agree.

SOPHIE

As I rode my bike home from Girls Who Code the day of the initial brainstorm, unusual images raced through my mind:

period blood, used pads wrapped in toilet paper, old blood-stained underwear. I felt giddy about the prospect of opening a conversation about a topic I had until now felt embarrassed to talk about. My years of embarrassment about my period turned to anger as I biked uptown. I was angry that I had been socialized to hide something that was such a natural part of my body and my life. How could I have been taught to be embarrassed by my period? And why? Period blood wasn't embarrassing or gross or crude. It is essential to human life and it churned inside my body, dribbling out of me every twenty days or so, faithfully staining at least one pair of underwear each month. Period blood was normal, beautiful even. So why wasn't I proud of it? After biking home and thinking more about the taboo, I felt physically excited to make the game, to turn it from just an idea to a reality.

Before this, most ideas I had about making something real and cool and innovative ended there. The "wouldn't it be funny if this existed?" or "I could really use something like that" stage happens all the time for me, and I think for most people. But so does the next stage: convincing myself that I'm not capable of making my idea into a reality or that it's too hard or that I don't have time or that I don't know where to start, so I just forget about it and move on. I was constantly putting my ideas down, assuming they weren't worth pursuing in larger, public ways. But with this idea I didn't have the option to succumb to that second stage. I couldn't give up because, in seven days, I had to have something to show.

There was something else different about this situation. Whereas some of my ideas make me laugh or find their way into the pages of my journal, this one made me feel physically giddy. It made me feel impassioned and jittery, like I couldn't wait to tell anyone within a foot of my face about the period game Andy and I had thought of. I wanted to start working on the game as soon as I got home, to put that passion into action. I wasn't a skilled enough coder yet to do that on my own in a single night, but there was something I *could* do. While my JavaScript skills were still a little shaky, there was one language I was fluent in: English.

When I got to my apartment I burst through the door, letting it slam behind me.

"How was your day?" my mom called out. (She had recently launched her own production company and was running it out of our apartment, like many start-ups, so she and two employees would sit around our dining-room table working all day.)

"Good, I'll tell you about it in a sec," I yelled as I ran down the long hallway to my room. I had to write. I had to channel all the thoughts that had been racing through my mind during the bike ride; I had to capture them on the page before my head exploded. I had relied on writing my whole life as a means of expression when other outlets felt uncomfortable or scary. Now, like putting on a favorite pair of shoes, I felt comfortable and good expressing my ideas this way.

Everything in my room became white noise as my fingers pelted the keyboard, rushing, rushing with desperation to get the sentences out of my head. Then, what felt like no time later, my fingers stopped moving. I slumped in my chair and stared at the screen, the blank white document now littered with black. I had written a loaded paragraph.

I read it out loud once, in a whisper. Then again a bit louder. Then again at full volume for the empty room.

> Most women menstruate for a large portion of their lives. It is, by all means, normal. Yet most people, women and men alike, feel uncomfortable talking about anything having to do with menstruation. The taboo that surrounds it teaches women that a normal and natural bodily function is embarrassing and crude. Our game is a way of discussing the taboo in an accessible way. Instead of holding a gun, the runner holds tampons, and instead of shooting enemies, the runner throws tampons at them. Although the concept of the video game may be strange, it's stranger that our society has accepted and normalized guns and violence through video games, yet we still find tampons and menstruation unspeakable. Hopefully one day menstruation will be as normal, if not more so, than guns and violence

have become in our society; normal enough to place in a video game without a second thought.

I felt proud of what I had written and dazed that it had come so quickly and naturally. I didn't even feel the need to revise it. If only every essay came to me so easily. If only everything I did happened in this creative, frenzied state. Now I understood what Laura Arrillaga-Andreessen had meant when she told us about the power of finding and pursuing our passions. I was not one to speak up inside or outside the classroom. But I had discovered a topic I felt so strongly about that I was ready for my voice, my opinion, to be heard. We could incorporate this paragraph into the game as a preamble before the user began to play. When they pressed the Start button, they would first go to a page with the statement and then launch into actual game play. That way the game would have a context to convey our larger message about the menstrual taboo. Using my writing to take a stand in this way felt like another important step on the road to finding my voice. Now I was just hoping that voice would be able to find an outlet.

BUILDING *TAMPON RUN*:
WE BANG OUR HEADS AND
MESS UP A LOT

ANDY

The next morning Sophie and I sat in the IAC conference room, anxious that we might not get the okay to move forward with our game. "If we need more evidence to validate our idea, I found something ridiculous," Sophie said, pulling up an article from the *Huffington Post* with a headline I thought must be a joke: "Tampons Confiscated, Guns Still Allowed at Texas Capitol Ahead of Abortion Vote."

Officials were concerned that women were going to use tampons or maxi pads as projectiles during the vote. But, don't worry, they were still allowing people to bring their guns into a state government building! As ridiculous as it was, this was the linchpin of our argument—and another sign that we were on the right track with our game.

Fortunately Reshma agreed we were on to something. She is an outspoken, visionary woman whose mission is to empower girls and give us the confidence and tools to achieve our full potential. Sophie and I were ecstatic when Sean told us that Reshma gave us the thumbs-up to build our potentially controversial game as our final project. Inspired by the ludicrous Texas capitol story, we named it *Texas Tampon Massacre*. But now we were faced with the actual task of making the game, and with a super-short deadline: seven days. We had to be finished by the Tuesday of the following week and ready to present it to about a hundred people at the Girls Who Code graduation that Wednesday.

I wasn't just worried about the timeline. Once we did finish our game, there would be another obstacle I had to face, and a much more personal one: showing *Texas Tampon Massacre* to my parents. I knew they would be at graduation day, but I wasn't sure I was ready for them to see the game. As soon as I was old enough to stop finger-painting and collaging at school, I never showed my work to my parents. It just wasn't our dynamic. My sisters didn't either. As long as we got good grades, they assumed our essays and projects were fine and so there was no need to review them. *Texas Tampon*

Massacre was the most far-fetched, out-there, politically charged thing I had ever done. I had no idea how my parents were going to react to the game, and I didn't want to find out. Maybe they would be confused and reject it outright? Or maybe they wouldn't like that I had spent the summer making a video game, instead of something less recreational? Or maybe they just wouldn't agree with what *Texas Tampon Massacre* stood for? The more I thought about it, the more my worries grew, threatening to spiral out of control. But I had to stop thinking about it. I was building a project that I really believed in, a project that Sophie and I needed to work hard on to get it into great shape before graduation day. Whenever my resolve wavered, I thought back to the speakers who had shared all their wisdom with us, including Reshma and Nikki, my Obi-Wan Kenobi. They both told me that it was okay to face change, be different, and break any mold that society tried to fit me into. I knew I was going to find success doing what I was passionate about, and I sure as hell knew I was passionate about *Texas Tampon Massacre*.

We had a mile-long list of things to do, and worrying about my parents wasn't one of them. For now, the game was distraction enough. Before we could write the code or design and create the visual elements, we had to map out the concept for the game. We knew that we were going to make a side-scroller where you can throw tampons at enemies. But who were those enemies going to be? Who was going to throw the tampons? What would we use to measure how well a user did? Were there going to be levels to the game, or was it going to scroll infinitely, like *Temple Run*? Before we got to do any actual programming, we had a lot to figure out.

After lengthy discussion and research, we decided the user would control a girl sitting on the left side of the screen. Enemies, dressed as cops (a nod toward the Texas tampon-confiscation incident), would run across the screen toward the girl. If a cop made contact with the girl, he would steal two tampons from her. To defend herself, the girl could throw tampons at the enemies. If she hit an enemy with a tampon, he would disappear. Tampon boxes would float across the screen, and the girl could jump to reload her ammo. If she ran out of tampons, the game would be over. Before the game play, we'd have a preamble describing the menstrual taboo and giving context to the game. If we had time, we'd design different avatars or characters that the user could choose to play as.

At the beginning, we kept biting off more than we could chew. It took a while for us to understand what goals were realistic, and what goals were impossible. I thought I could make the characters animate in a morning, and Sophie thought she could make the girl jump in that same amount of time. And at first we never met our goals. Luckily, at the beginning of the project Sean had told every team to figure out an MVP (otherwise known as a minimum viable product)—basically, our worst-case-scenario project. If it came down to it, what is the simplest thing that Sophie and I could develop that could convey our concept and that we could present on graduation day? Our MVP was creating a rectangle that represented the girl and rectangles to represent the enemies. The girl rectangle would spew black squares (which represented tampons), and the enemy rectangle would disappear on impact with either the girl or the tampons. If we could program this in a week, we would be able to use it to describe our hopes for a fully designed, fully executed *Texas Tampon Massacre*. But while it was comforting to have an MVP, Sophie and I knew that we wouldn't be satisfied with just that. We were determined to build and design a completely rendered game in the few days we had.

The first step was to map out where the girl and her enemies would be placed on the screen and how they would move. We represented our heroine with a blue rectangle, and the enemies with orange rectangles. Sophie and I sat coding our MVP together, watching as the white screen became littered with blue and orange rectangles colliding together and disappearing (the collisions were quick to code because I had experience from the *Odyssey* game).

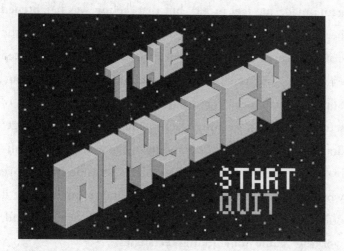

I loved the feeling of watching our game come together on-screen, even if it was an extremely basic version. I felt triumphant knowing that everything happening in front of us was because of code Sophie and I had written.

I had been used to flying solo, but I came to appreciate Sophie as a collaborator more and more. We both brought such different ideas and perspectives to the table. We inspired each other, building off the other person's ideas about the game's message and how to tackle our code, making our ideas better and stronger. During the week of final projects, we became very close, not just as project partners, but as friends. We jammed out to music, popped popcorn, walked to the subway together (when she didn't bike), and got to know each other really well—it made the experience of creating *Texas Tampon Massacre* so much richer. Building the game made me feel proud, but that feeling was heightened because I could share it with Sophie. Sophie also played the critical role of being our project manager. I get distracted easily and lose track of time—Sophie balanced me out. Sophie is extremely organized and did an incredible job of setting priorities, keeping track of the tasks we had to get done each day, and understanding when we had to recalibrate our schedule and priorities. She kept us on track as we worked toward completing the MVP, and to our surprise it only took us two days. By the end of day three, we had a full, working "game" of colliding rectangles.

We sat staring at our colliding rectangles, mesmerized by our creation. "It's beautiful," Sophie whispered. Other girls, packing up their stuff for the day, gathered around our computer. "It's so cool!" they said as they crowded behind us. It's funny that something so simple could make us all so excited.

With the remaining time we had, we knew it would be best to divide and conquer, tackling different parts of the game we still had to make. Now we were ready for the design phase: turning the blue and orange rectangles into actual characters. When Sophie and I had first discussed what the game was going to look like, we stared at each other, daring the other to make the art. Neither of us was confident enough in our skills to commit to making art for a full project. Then it hit me. Pixel art. Pixel art, similar to what old games like *Super Mario Bros.* looked like, was much easier to animate than traditional art. It has a lot less detail. For example, imagine a smiley face. A black pixel could represent an eye. To make that smiley face wink, I'd just make the eye a few pixels longer.

Some of the game art would have to be animated, like the girl's and the enemies' running, moving legs. Since I had animated pixel art before, I offered to tackle the art and the animation. Sophie, who was helping code other aspects of the game, offered at this point to tackle getting the girl to jump so she could evade her tampon-stealing enemies and also so that she could reach the tampon boxes that sometimes floated above her to refuel her ammunition. Little did we know, those two tasks would push us both to our limits.

SOPHIE

While the manifesto at the opening of the game felt effortless to write, I had a lot more difficulty "writing" other parts. That was partially because I was using a new language, JavaScript, to express myself. That meant that Andy and I had to break down anything we wanted to see on-screen into code: a conditional statement or a loop or the two combined. And since this was our own project, we had no guidelines or handout from Sean to help us.

On the fourth day, feeling like hot shit after finishing our MVP, it was time for me to get the main girl to jump so she could dodge enemies and get tampon boxes. At this point Andy had designed an actual girl to take the place of the blue rectangle. If the game was sort of like a big Cartesian plane, all I was doing was changing her y-coordinate on the press of the Up arrow on the keyboard. I didn't think this task would even take me to the next hour. I didn't know it yet, but I was so horribly wrong.

Side by side, Andy and I pounded away at our computers. Just as they had when I wrote the preamble, my fingers flew across the keyboard with the flow of knowing what you need to do and diving into doing it. And then, half an hour later, I was done. I sat back and smiled, looking at the fifteen lines of code I had written.

```
if (keycode == 38) {
    jump();
}

void jump() {
    while (player.yCoordinate > 300) {
        player.yCoordinate = player.yCoordinate − 20;
    }
    fall();
}

void fall() {
    while (player.yCoordinate < 400) {
        player.yCoordinate = player.yCoordinate + 20;
    }
}
```

Now I just had to make sure my code actually worked. I pulled up the game with the elements we had created so far and pressed the Up arrow. Nothing. Wait, what? Nothing! The girl didn't move. I pressed the button again. Nothing. Again. Nothing. Again. I watched her run, but she wasn't going up and she wasn't going back down.

Whyyyyyyyy? I whined in my head. I felt like the human incarnation of the Y U NO WORK meme. I slumped in my chair. This was supposed to be simple, just a change in the girl's y-coordinate, but I didn't see her y-coordinate changing. I took a deep breath and ate some of Andy's popcorn. It had only been a half hour. I could figure this out. I would figure this out.

Maybe it was a problem with the Up key on my keyboard. If the code wasn't registering the Up key, then of course she wouldn't be jumping.

```
if (keycode == 38) {
    System.out.println("up key pressed");
    jump();
}
```

I now had to figure out if the problem was with the Up registering, or with the jump code. I was hoping the key was the problem because that would be easy to fix. All I would have to do is find the typo or comb through the documentation for a different way to respond to key touches. But if, on the other hand, my jump code wasn't working, that meant I would have to completely rethink how I was approaching writing the code. I was frustrated, confused, and overwhelmed by the idea of scrapping everything I had written so far and starting over. I couldn't even imagine how else I would approach jumping other than what I'd already thought of.

I ran the code again, hoping not to see "up key pressed"

in the console, since that would mean the problem was with my jump code. But life doesn't always work out the way you want. I pressed the Up key and "up key pressed" popped up in the console. That meant that the computer was recognizing the command to press the Up button, but again the girl didn't jump. I pressed the Up key again and again and "up key pressed" continued to print to the console. Those three words haunted me. Clearly my jump code wasn't working.

"Is everything okay?" Andy asked as I sat there with my face scrunched into a sour ball, my finger repeatedly pressing the Up button.

"It's not working. She's not jumping and the problem isn't with the Up key."

"Do you need to talk it out?"

"Not yet." I told Andy I was probably just missing something small or had made a typo somewhere. There were still two more hours until lunch; I could figure it out on my own.

"Well, let me know if you do," she said, then pushed her headphones back on and disappeared into her own world of code.

I was determined to get this to work. With two summers more of coding experience under her belt, Andy was objectively the better coder of the two of us. While I struggled over small tasks, Andy breezed through major ones. While I sat there close to tears with frustration, she bopped her head to music and ate popcorn. In the hour I had spent struggling to get the girl to jump, Andy had gotten the score working and was now on to the next task. I'd never been this person on a team before. In (dreaded) group projects at school, I was the one who ended up doing all the work, sometimes because no one else was doing it and sometimes because I only trusted myself to get it done. Now I was the person on the team who was weighing us down, who couldn't get the job done. I could imagine Andy sitting around the dinner table at home telling her parents, "The girl I'm working with is so bad at coding! I'm doing all the work. It's so annoying."

I was determined to figure out how to make the girl jump by myself, but it was also comforting to know that Andy was by my side, there to fall back on if I really couldn't get it. With a little time, she'd probably be able to figure out the bug in my code or talk out a new way to approach jumping.

I read over the fifteen lines of jump code, looking for a bug. Once over, then twice over, then three times over, and I still couldn't figure out why it wasn't working. I traced what the code was doing with my hands in the air and I still couldn't figure it out. "This should be working!" I felt like screaming to the nineteen other girls around the table. So I got some water, ate some more popcorn, stretched—and even after all of that, I still couldn't figure it out.

"Wanna eat lunch now?" Andy asked.

"Now?"

"Yeah, it's twelve and I'm hungry." She rummaged in her bag, first for a sandwich and then for another bag of popcorn to pop in the microwave.

How had two hours flown by? In that time I had written only fifteen lines of code, and they didn't even work, and I didn't know why. I wanted to pull out my hair and then rip the torn hair into smaller shreds and then throw the shreds on the floor and stomp on them. I wanted to throw something (or maybe even someone) out the window.

"Taking your mind off it and eating will help," Andy prodded. I don't think she knew that I had already tried the taking-your-mind-off-it tactic with unsuccessful results, but I still welcomed a new distraction. While I consumed leftover dinner, I continued to press the Up button, hoping somehow the girl would miraculously start to jump . . . but she just kept running in place. I hated her. Look at her shit-eating grin and abnormally large head. She was deceptively adorable, a stubborn monster who inflicted pain on human beings. It was her fault she wasn't jumping. She was inflicting pain on me.

I spent the next four hours changing number values and adding printlines. It was like I was just changing numbers in an equation when really I had to change the equation itself. But I had no ideas and I was getting more and more frustrated. She wouldn't jump. *I'm just bad at coding.* She wouldn't jump. *I hate coding.* She wouldn't jump. *I have to figure this out.* I was not only mad at myself for not getting the code to work (and mad at the computer and the world), but I felt, even more intensely than I had before, like I was letting Andy down. We only had a few more days left to finish the project and I had wasted a whole seven hours on something that I anticipated should have taken me only one.

"I'm going to stay late," I told her as she packed up to leave. "I'm so sorry jump is taking so long."

"Don't worry about it," she told me. "You'll get it eventually." But what else was she going to say?

Sean and I spent the next half hour talking about jumping. "What happens if you press the Up button while she's in the air? How quickly is her y-coordinate changing? Do you need to only have one method or is there another way you could do this?" he asked. I hadn't thought about those questions yet. Coding requires you to think about a problem at its most basic level, to make no assumptions, to create steps for your solution little by little, and I was still learning to think in this foreign way.

By the time I left the Ice Cream Cake that day, my eyes turning to balls of mush, my mind focused on going up and down, I was desperate for the answer. I felt like a starving animal sniffing around for a dead carcass. I knew it was close, but where was it? "What am I missing?" I asked my bike lock and my bungee cord and then secured my backpack onto the back of the bike. And then suddenly everything clicked.

Oh my . . . I realized that she was probably just jumping too quickly so I couldn't see her actually going up and down. I had to slow her down and, oh my . . . I could use a variable to check whether she was already in the air or back down on the ground and, oh my . . . I had to get this all out of my head and into reality. I unstrapped the bungee, pulled out my notebook, and my fingers scrawled desperately across the page with a worn-down pencil, filling the whiteness with code as I stood slouched on a street corner, the city moving around me. I felt like taking a victory lap around the block. I could have hugged a stranger.

The next morning I got to the Ice Cream Cake early and sat at my computer pounding away at the keyboard, tuning out the rest of the world. The new code flowed out of me, just as the preamble had a few days before. When I finished, I took a deep breath. "This must be it," my right brain said. "Don't get your hopes up," my left brain responded. So I ran the code, and the window with the game popped up, and my body felt tingly with anticipation, my finger hovering on the Up button. "Please, please, I will give you my firstborn child, please jump!" I whispered, and then I pushed my finger down.

My jaw dropped and I flung my hands in the air, rolled the chair behind me, twirled, gave myself a high five, and released a very loud "YEEEESSSSSSS!" She had done it. She had finally jumped. And I had done it. I had made her jump. I was still pressing the button when Andy walked in.

"Look!" I pressed it for her and the girl went up and she went back down. "Isn't that incredible?!" I pressed it again and again, mesmerized by her movements. I had made that happen. I had figured it out. I had coded that.

"Awesome!" Andy said. "I knew you'd get it eventually."

"I'm really sorry again that it took me so long."

"Really, don't worry about it! I just feel bad it was so frustrating."

So she wasn't mad? She didn't think I was a deadweight team member? Maybe this was real collaboration and all those school group projects had been a pretend version. I realized that good collaboration means building up your team members and trusting them to accomplish difficult tasks, like what Andy was doing for me. Instead of simply doing all the coding herself because she was more adept at it, or making me feel bad for struggling, she was trusting and supporting me. And now that I had accomplished jumping, I had her to share the excitement with. Working with her on the project also meant that even when I was most frustrated, giving up wasn't an option. I was accountable not only to myself but to her as well.

I sat there continuously pressing Up, beaming at the computer. All the frustration of the day before was gone. In fact, the frustration only made the success feel better. It felt incredible to write the preamble, to feel so passionate that the whole paragraph just flew out of me. But failing and trying and failing and trying until I finally figured out how to get the girl to jump was even more rewarding. I had become a better coder through the process, and I had also experienced firsthand that whenever we try to do anything that is challenging and new, we might fail at first, but that's the only way to grow and learn. It's okay not to get the right answer immediately. It doesn't mean I'm not good at coding or I'm dumb, it just means that I have to keep working at it until I figure it out. I still feel proud when I watch the girl jump. With her beautiful smile and track-star legs and my eventually masterful coding, she gracefully moves up and down.

ANDY

Sophie wasn't the only one to hit a roadblock. My task was to design and animate the girl, who we'd dubbed Luna, a nod to the connection between menstrual cycles and lunar cycles. At first, I thought animating Luna would be easy. Designing her, I'd been inspired by figures from games from the eighties with low-resolution detail: rectangles for limbs, black squares for eyes, and a limited color palette. Now I had to get my little eighties lady to look like she was running. But how? Animation works by taking multiple images and rapidly alternating between them to create the illusion of movement. Each set of images, or objects in the game, is called a sprite. Seems simple, right? Well, I spent more time figuring out how to actually code the animation than any other part of the game.

Thursday night, I coded late into the night on my bed, only crawling out of my room to use the bathroom, get a drink, or get snacks. Like I had with the *Odyssey*, I turned to the internet for help. The World Wide Web was up 24/7, always ready to answer any question I had. So I searched and searched and searched. The coding community loves to ask for help, and they also love to give it. There are countless forums online with folks offering snippets of their own code to the programmer in need. As the night stretched on, I trucked through the muck of ways other people had used code to get a sprite to animate. I followed one set of advice, then another. But the context in which they were animating images wasn't the same as mine. All the coding forums I found sort of helped—but nothing I did worked. It was torture. Animating Luna should have been so easy, so simple. But she refused to move. If I could figure this out for

Luna, I could figure it out for everything else: the enemies, the tampons, the tampon boxes. But nothing worked! *Nothing* worked! NOTHING WORKED! I felt like I spent all night banging my head against a wall. I took all the tutorials, clicked through each of their pages, pulling code and coding concepts that I thought were relevant to the girl's animation. Piece by piece, line by line, the right program came together. At about three o'clock in the morning I passed out exhausted, everything a blurry fog. When I woke up the next morning I ran the code in a panic, anxious that I wouldn't have anything to show Sophie that day. But to my relief, my hard work paid off—Luna sprinted across our endlessly scrolling background, arms pumping, hair flowing.

At GWC later that day, I showed Sophie our fully functioning Luna, running and jumping and lunging to throw tampons. We had our girl! Reenergized by the small but very significant improvement to our game, Sophie and I dove into the remaining tasks. We started by planning the screen flow for game play. First, the Start screen. Then, the Preamble screen. Then, the Instruction screen, the actual game screen, and finally, a Game Over screen with the score the user reached. Sophie started working on the code to get the game to progress from screen to screen, and I began creating art for the rest of the game and plugging it into the code. Our game suddenly felt like it was falling into place—we weren't done just yet, but it wasn't an abstract idea anymore.

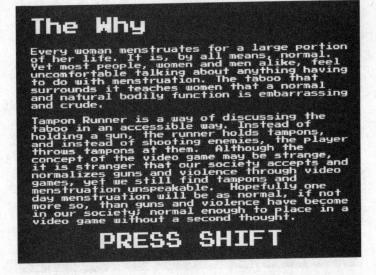

By Tuesday, we stepped back from our computer screens and admired the Start screen we had built informing the player of the menstrual taboo. We also admired the game, watching the girl run, fling tampons, and jump. Enemies zoomed across the screen. In the corner, numbers ticked as the girl lost tampons and defeated enemies. If someone had said that Sophie and I would create a full-fledged video game in a week, including research, a pitch, and a developed social message, I never would have believed it. With careful planning and hard work, we were able to complete the game. All we needed now was a title that people would take seriously.

Texas Tampon Massacre sounded gory, I knew, but my terrible sense of humor led me to believe this was an amazing working title. But Sophie and I knew it wasn't the right tone for the satirical social-issue game we had created. As we

racked our brains, someone in the Girls Who Code group suggested *Tampon Run*. Sophie and I faced each other, repeating "Tampon Run" over and over and over again to see if it would stick. It became a chant: "Tampon Run . . . Tampon Run . . . Tampon Run . . ." The more I repeated it, the better it felt. It was just right for our game.

The next day we would unveil Luna and our game to a room full of people at the Girls Who Code graduation ceremony. I had nervous déjà vu from the day of unveiling my *Odyssey* game to my English class: I wondered how people would react to our head-on embrace of menstruation, tampons, and period talk . . . especially my parents.

8

WE S#*T OUR PANTS (VERY NERVOUS)

SOPHIE

My shaking hands were making my bike zigzag as I rode down to the Ice Cream Cake that Wednesday. It was the morning of the Girls Who Code graduation, which meant that in eight hours Andy and I would be presenting our completed final project to a crowd of strangers: people who worked at IAC as well as the parents and siblings of the other girls from Girls Who Code. I entered the lobby to find a small stage with rows and rows of chairs for the audience. A stage?!

I was excited to unveil *Tampon Run* to the world, to get to say the words "menstruation" and "tampon" openly and proudly to a room of people. But I was equally (actually, more) nervous to get on a stage and speak to a large group. As the weeks had passed at Girls Who Code, my "only raise my hand when no one else answers the question" rule turned into a "whenever I know the correct answer" rule and then a "whenever I think I know the correct answer" rule, which really meant I could raise my hand whenever. Raising my hand had never been a choice before. This was new and big. It was fun to be heard. I discovered I had a voice and now I really wanted to use it.

But all that newfound confidence disappeared when I walked through the door the morning of graduation. I couldn't keep my limbs from feeling like they were floating around my body at the sight of the stage. I was sweating. I knew I should have packed deodorant. Would people like the game or would no one take us seriously? Or, worse, would people feel uncomfortable? We weren't just presenting for our eighteen friends in the IAC conference room. Now we would be sharing our idea with a bunch of adult strangers, people who wouldn't be supportive no matter what. People who might hate our project. The stakes felt so much higher.

But I had to keep going about my day, taking the now familiar elevator up to the conference room and trying to remain calm.

When Andy arrived at IAC later that morning, I found out she hadn't even begun to memorize or practice our *Tampon*

Run presentation. The result: me quietly freaking out on the inside. I insisted that we had to practice until we had it down, which meant doing it over and over. We headed to the bathroom, our presentation practice space of choice.

"I feel like we've practiced enough," Andy said a few hours later. "I'm going to go eat lunch." She walked toward the door of the bathroom.

"Wait! Andy!" And then it all came out, fears and anxieties spilling from my mouth. How nervous I was for this presentation, how it was more than butterflies in my stomach, how it was sweating and lightheadedness and blurry vision and wishing with all of my being that I was anywhere but here. How this had been a problem ever since I could remember, how I had gone to a speaking circle a few months before to try to fix it, how I knew my intense fear of being perceived as dumb and incompetent was irrational but I couldn't help it. How I felt like our presentation needed to be perfect so I would feel less nervous to get on the stage and share our ideas.

We stood for a moment in silence in the white-tiled bathroom. I couldn't believe I had just told this girl, who I liked a lot but barely knew, all about my internal ugliness. Now she knew more about me than some of my friends at school. Now she could see who I really was: an unconfident, insecure, scared person.

"I didn't realize that when you said you were nervous you

meant all of that," Andy said after a moment. "If practicing more is gonna make you feel better, then let's do it!"

And for the first time that day, I felt myself relax.

I had put myself and my needs on the table. I had spoken up, and it paid off. Andy was my friend and she was my collaborator. We were a team. And just as Andy had done when I struggled to get Luna to jump, teammates support each other to work through obstacles, to learn from those challenges, and to succeed. This was a small step in becoming the person I aspired to be, but at least I was moving forward.

Still, saying all my feelings out loud in the bathroom didn't mean all my nerves had disappeared. They continued to sit heavily on my body. At lunch I copied my lines onto a notecard (aka a piece of white card-stock scrap lying on the table) to bring onstage with me.

"You don't really need that. You memorized your lines," Andy said when she saw it, trying to be encouraging and supportive.

"Yeah, but you never know."

"You're not going to forget your lines on stage. You know them, it's going to be great."

But her words didn't console me.

The hours passed, families and IAC employees filed in, and then it was five thirty, time for the ceremony to begin. I watched pair after pair get up on stage and zip through their presentations. They made it look so easy. We were slated to go last, which only prolonged my inevitable doom.

I sat in total fear as the girls who created an app about different hairstyles presented, followed by two girls who displayed an app that generated different art for different songs. And then I heard the words I had been dreading: "Next we have Andrea Gonzales and Sophie Houser of *Tampon Run*."

There was applause and confused laughter. "Tampon Run" had taken the audience by surprise; I could feel in the energy of the room that they were interested to hear what we had to say. Andy and I gave each other a "we got this, let's go talk about our periods" look, and for a moment I considered leaving my notecard on my chair. I was ready; I was going to do great. I didn't need a safety net.

But I couldn't let go of my notecard.

"Let's go," Andy whispered as I clutched the piece of white card stock like it was my teddy bear, Fluffy, on the first day of kindergarten.

Andy began the speech I had heard so many times that day, the speech I had written for us the night before. "Every woman menstruates" flowed into my right ear and 140 strange eyes looked at me and seventy lips laughed at the word "tampon," and my mind felt like the bubbles in a glass of seltzer rising up, up, up. I was taking in the world, but I wasn't processing it. Everything looked whiter than it should and my hands were dampening the notecard they clutched tighter and tighter. I wanted to curl up in a ball in my bed and pull the covers over my head. Then there was silence; Andy's words weren't flowing into my right ear anymore. I turned to look at her and she stared back at me yelling "Your turn!" and yelling "Speak!" with her eyes, and I told my body "Your turn!" and told it "Speak!" and my mind responded, "I forgot all my lines."

Panic. Pure panic. I'm lucky that I can say this was maybe the most panic I've ever felt in one moment in my life. One hundred forty eyes stared at me and then the second phase of "I forgot all my lines while presenting to a bunch of strangers" set in. I felt myself smile. Was this really happening? And then phase three: I remembered the notecard. Thank you, Past Sophie, for holding on to this piece of paper. I love you.

I raised the damp white card stock, the edges mindlessly torn by my nervous hands, and attempted to scan the first bullet point. S#*t. I had not anticipated needing the help, so it was upside down. I lost another millisecond turning it around while 140 eyes continued to watch. All I could do to drag myself to the finish line two minutes away was read off the card, so that's what I did.

When we had finished explaining the menstrual taboo and our approach to combating it with a game, the audience applauded loudly and I felt my carbonated mind flatten again and my limbs loosen and my hands stop sweating. We smiled, said "thank you," and, on our way off the stage, high-fived.

"I forgot all my lines," I whispered to Andy.

"Whatever," she whispered back. "We did great!"

My body was warm and my mind was swimming, but I felt exhilarated. In all that excitement I was transported to the ski slopes on the first day of skiing every winter. I was always terrified during the first runs of the year, paralyzed by a fear of falling. In Dr. Graham's office a few months before I had told him about skiing. About how the last time I had skied, I became so scared of pointing my skis down the mountain, of moving, that the emergency team had to come pick me up in a snowmobile and take me to the bottom. But secretly, under the fear, I knew I needed to fall, because after the first tumble in the snow, skiing didn't seem scary anymore.

"I wish I had fallen down that time," I had told him, "because now I don't think I'll be able to ski again." We sat in silence. "And I wish I had thrown up once while presenting in class or lost my voice or forgotten all my lines, because then it wouldn't be so scary."

"Well, maybe one day you will," he told me.

"That scares me too."

But, finally, on an August evening in downtown Manhattan, I had fallen down in the snow and gotten up, put my skis back on, and raced down the mountain without the help of a snowmobile. Finally, the worst had happened. And with dozens of strangers watching!

When I walked off the stage and sat down in my chair, I beamed. I wanted to get up and stop the ceremony and shout to all 140 eyes, "I just now failed and I didn't die! Look at me, I'm alive! I did it!" Instead I sat still and silent and saved that for my parents after the ceremony ended. I knew I hadn't solved all my insecurities. I knew that the next time I got on a stage I'd be just as scared and sweaty as I had been earlier in the night. But at least I'd discovered that the worst possible situation wasn't actually so bad.

"Your presentation was great," my mom told me later.

"I forgot all my lines!"

"I didn't even notice. You shouldn't feel bad."

"No." She didn't understand. "I don't feel bad. This is so exciting!" For the next few hours I had that conversation over and over. Anyone who complimented our presentation got an exuberant "I forgot all my lines!"

Now I love notecards. They have a special place in my

heart thanks to that torn-up piece of card stock that saved me on graduation day. I have not forgotten my lines since, but I like knowing that if I ever do, I will have a strategy to fall back on. And I love knowing that if I ever do forget my lines again, contrary to what I previously believed, I won't spontaneously combust or die on the spot. The presentation will always go on.

That night when I got home I put this notecard in my folder of "special things" so I would have it forever.

ANDY

Unlike Sophie, I was not terribly nervous about getting up and speaking in front of a large crowd at graduation. But while I wasn't nervous about our presentation, I was definitely anxious about its aftereffects. Everyone at Girls Who Code knew that Sophie and I were making a game about the menstrual taboo, but my family certainly did not.

My family valued that we had dinner together every evening. We all talked about our days, yet it was never in much detail. In the final week and a half at Girls Who Code, I skirted around the details of my final project. I told them I was making a video game and nothing more.

"I'm working on it with a girl from Bard High School—Sophie Houser."

"It's a side-scrolling platformer."

"I'm focusing on the sprite animation, and Sophie's working on the jump function."

My family learned about *Tampon Run* on a need-to-know basis, and frankly, they didn't need to know much. When I was home working on *Tampon Run*, I'd hole myself up in my room. My parents would see me creeping around late at night during food breaks, and my sisters (who were a bit more informed, but not by much) would pop in and out while I wrestled with bugs in the code.

I told myself that I wasn't nervous about telling my family, I just didn't need their help. But even in all my pretend self-reliance, I knew in my gut that my unwillingness to share details wasn't just about working independently; there was something more. As much as we talked over the dinner table, my family never talked about periods. The only exception was one bathroom gathering where my mom explained how to use a pad and said NEVER to use tampons. We discussed menstruation as little as possible, only hastily mentioning our need for more pads and tampons (once we acclimated our mother to the prospect of using them). If I couldn't talk about periods in my own home, how could I be comfortable telling my family that I'm making a game about tampons?

So, fearing rejection and disapproval, I hid it. I was really excited about *Tampon Run*—but one negative word from my parents and I wouldn't be as happy working on it. I avoided the possibility entirely by keeping my mouth shut. And I guess they never technically asked if I was making a game where you throw tampons at people—that was excuse enough for me not to tell them. But with graduation getting closer by the hour, I couldn't avoid it for much longer.

On the day of graduation, we were told to put our poster boards—science fair-style presentations of our projects—on tables in the lobby. To my dismay, they were situated right at the entrance—people would see them before they seated themselves in front of the graduation stage. I turned to Elizabeth, one of our TAs.

"Doesn't this mean the audience will see the projects before we've pitched them?" I said, laughing nervously.

"Yeah, I think that's the point—not all the parents are coming at once. If they come early, they'll be able to check out the projects before the ceremony," she responded.

I panicked. My parents will see this before I present! They won't understand what I've been working on at all! No one will! Everyone will be totally repulsed, and they'll hate my project before I even get the chance to explain it to them!

After setting up the computers at our presentation table, I nervously adjusted the poster board. Across the top, it read *Tampon Run*, and in my anxiety, I felt like it stood out from everything else, blaring its name across the lobby. I wanted to hide—but there was no escaping this, and I knew it. As parents shuffled in, I scanned anxiously for mine. But as everyone took their seats, they were nowhere to be found. They finally rushed in a minute before the ceremony began, too late to even notice our poster board. I'd dodged a bullet, at least for now.

As Sophie and I walked on stage to present a half hour later, I couldn't take my eyes off my parents. They were sitting toward the front. I pictured them squirming with embarrassment as I talked about the menstrual taboo and, for a moment, I wished I didn't have to be up here. Was I about to become the disappointment of my family? I could tell by Sophie's flushed face and sweaty hands that she was feeling the same way, except I knew it was for different reasons. I gave her a smile and a nod, a silent "We got this," and then started our presentation.

When I delivered my opening, I looked over at my parents, and to my surprise, they didn't look uncomfortable at all. Maybe they were just hiding their humiliation? But I didn't have time to think about that, because it soon became apparent by the silence next to me that Sophie had forgotten her lines.

My heart stopped. I've made mistakes performing piano, but I had one golden rule: never stop playing. Even if I fumbled through a measure of music, coming to a full stop is much worse: you lose track of where you were, forget where to pick up again, and there goes all your momentum. The moments of Sophie's absolute silence seemed to stretch into eternity— if we didn't do something soon, it would be over. Sophie and I exchanged panicked glances while we figured out what to do next. Would she look at her notecard? Would I have to ad-lib? In that second, I desperately prayed for the former. I was trained in classical music, not jazz. I'm not good at improvising.

Everything seemed to move in slow motion while Sophie lifted the notecard in her hand, rotated it, and began reading. I almost passed out with relief. Before I knew it, the two and a half minutes had passed, and applause rang from the audience, adrenaline still pumping through my veins. In a daze, Sophie and I high-fived and returned to our seats, my green Doc Martens clomping across the stage and down the steps. I had only seen a glimpse of my parents' reactions to the pitch, and I nervously waited until the end of the ceremony to see how they felt.

Afterward, we proceeded to our poster boards to answer questions from the audience and eat fancy sandwiches. People were already at our station, waiting for us to set up the game demos for them.

Everybody and their moms (literally) stopped by, either to

give congratulations, play *Tampon Run*, or ask us questions about the project and the menstrual taboo. I laughed, smiled, did all the small talk. The response to our project was incredible; I never expected such a positive reaction. But between bites of my sandwich and chats with passersby, I anxiously waited for my parents to stop by the booth.

And soon enough, my mama and papa came over, plates piled high with sandwiches and drinks. "Hey, hon!" my mom said. "We came late but we ran in and caught your presentation!"

"Hi," I answered. There was silence as my parents smiled at me and my poster board, munching on their food. I waited for them to say something more. I waited, and waited, and waited. I hastily exchanged pleasantries with a nearby couple, but nothing could divert my attention from my parents, still smiling and peering at our board.

"Want some food?" My dad pushed the plate in my direction, and I grabbed something random: chicken, goat cheese, greens.

I tried eating some of the food, but quickly blurted out, "Wafgh digh you phfink?" Crumbs spewed from my mouth.

"Oh, we loved it!"

I gasped, swallowing the rest of my food. "Really?"

"Yeah. We're so proud of you!" my dad said.

My mom continued. "I was a bit weirded out when I saw the poster board earlier, but it makes sense. It was great."

They were all smiles, totally oblivious to how shocked I was.

"Where's Sean? We should say hi." They hugged me and hurried off.

I was stunned—they were unfazed! I turned to Sophie. "They liked it!"

"They liked it?"

"THEY LIKED IT!"

For the second time that day, Sophie and I slammed our hands together in the highest of fives. I technically can only speak for myself, but I think it's safe to say we both felt great.

For the rest of the night, we mingled with our classmates, their parents, and other visitors. The food slowly disappeared, the ice in the drink cooler melted, and the sun set. At the end of the night, I hopped into the car with my parents, vibrating with excitement, exhaustion, and relief. All our hard work paid off, and everyone loved what we did. Even my parents.

I almost texted Sophie to congratulate ourselves, but I felt nothing was as appropriate as Snapchatting her an exuberant "WE DID IT!"

We really had. But as we zoomed up the West Side High-way back toward the Bronx, I couldn't help feeling a little guilty. My parents had reacted so positively toward *Tampon Run*, and all this time I had assumed that they would reject it. I was annoyed—not because they disliked my final proj-ect, but because I'd been so quick to judge them. I looked at my parents from the backseat: my dad drove the car, quietly humming; my mom was listening to a podcast on her phone, trying to learn French again. I knew I loved them a lot, and I knew that they were sometimes unfair to me—but maybe I acted a little unfairly toward them too.

But, while the *Tampon Run* unveiling went much better than I expected, I wasn't ready to drive off into the sunset just yet.

. . . Mostly because I'd forgotten my jacket back at IAC.

9

SOME REAL WISH FULFILLMENT

SOPHIE

Andy and I had made *Tampon Run* as good as we could in the seven days we worked on it at Girls Who Code. But after the program ended, we were so excited that we wanted to keep working and make the game even better. We planned to do everything in our power to get *Tampon Run* into the wider world. After all, how could it change the menstrual taboo if no one saw it?

Before Girls Who Code, if I had created something I was proud of, like a short story or a movie, I never would have shown it to anyone other than maybe my mom. Sharing my creative endeavors scared me. It was the same thing as my issues around raising my hand in class and expressing my ideas. I assumed that whatever I created was bad, or at least wasn't better than what anyone else made. So if I showed it to people, I was saying I thought it was good—which was extra embarrassing if they didn't like it. But after a summer of getting up and presenting my projects, from the slot machine to scrolling rectangles to *Tampon Run*, I discovered it was actually kind of fun to present my work. It felt great to watch people take an interest in what I created and, to my surprise, all the girls in the program and everyone at graduation had reacted positively to my projects. In fact, at graduation I also saw how fulfilling it was to talk about something as "off-limits" and uncomfortable as my period, much more so than talking about something normal. There was a real thrill to it. Most of the audience members were eager to hear and talk about menstruation and the taboo precisely because they'd always felt awkward around the subject. People love having an outlet to talk about topics they feel forced to keep inside, as long as the outlet is nonthreatening and fun, which *Tampon Run* was. So I was eager to continue experiencing that nervous but exciting rush of showing people something I had worked hard on and was proud of, and also something that gave me and other people the opportunity to be uninhibited. I was ready to show *Tampon Run* to the world.

One requirement of the graduation-day presentation had been listing hypothetical next steps on the project. Whereas other groups talked about possible new features, Andy and I thought even further into the future and put together a list of blogs that might write up the game. We chose blogs we thought would be interested in our message about the menstrual taboo, and told ourselves that we'd know we made it if Jezebel, an online feminist news outlet, covered us. In our wildest fantasies, we dreamed that *Tampon Run* would become the next *Flappy Bird*. We imagined it going viral. I mean, we also had literally no idea how to actually get it out there and make all that happen. But we had put in so much time and energy, it felt like the only option was to try.

Andy and I spent the week after the program touching up the game and adding features. Instead of working at IAC, we'd sit around my dining-room table or at a nearby bubble tea place, or just communicate over email.

It was incredible that, even though we came from such different backgrounds and approached things so differently, we had formed such a deep bond over the past few weeks of working together. We made each other laugh and had fun like I did with my school friends. But we shared something else as well: we inspired each other, feeding off each other's ideas, humor, and unique ways of seeing the world. Since I felt so comfortable around Andy at that point, I didn't feel scared to suggest any idea, no matter how weird. That's how people can be really creative and innovative in their thinking, feeling like they don't need to censor their thoughts. But since we were collaborators and friends, I also felt comfortable telling her whenever I thought a concept for the game or the website or the launch plan wasn't working.

When, a week later, Andy sent over the code with the final touches (fun animations for the intro slides and making your number of tampons flash red when it got low), I wrote her back maybe one of the nicest things I've said to anyone ever: "Thank you so much. Bravo. I cannot express it enough. I want to bake you a cake of love and then throw it at you."

The next step was uploading *Tampon Run* to a website. I had no idea how to do this, so I turned to the most knowledgeable presence in my life: Google. As I typed in "buying a url" and clicked on the first link, a site called GoDaddy, I couldn't stop thinking how crazy it was that we were actually doing this. None of the other girls in the program had continued to work on their projects or pursued releasing them into the world.

So here I was, poking around GoDaddy, trying to find the "domain" section, which I learned was a fancy word for URL. I sat at my desk in momentary terror as I checked whether the "tamponrun.com" domain name was already claimed. It was available and for only $14.99 a year it was mine for the taking. Poking around some more, I learned I also had to buy something called "hosting" to host the things I actually wanted on the site. Twenty-five dollars poorer and a half hour later, we had a live, working (albeit extremely simple) website where people could play the game. Who cared that the page was mostly white space? It looked like a masterpiece to me. I couldn't believe that all it took to get a website working was pressing a few buttons and punching in my credit card information. "LOOK IT'S REAL," I chatted Andy and then sent her the link. I spent the next half hour playing the game, sitting alone in my room virtually throwing tampons, jumping for tampon boxes, and bouncing to Beethoven's *Moonlight* Sonata (the 8-bit version is *Tampon Run*'s background music). I couldn't believe that Andy and I had thought up this game and then actually built it and now I was sitting here in my room playing it on a real website on the real, live internet.

After finalizing and uploading the game, the third step—and the most difficult one—was actually getting people to see it. We made a Google doc titled "Releasing *Tampon Run* like Blood from the Uterus" and then created a list of speakers to send the game to, celebrities to tweet it at, and sites we could submit it to. Throughout the week, Andy and I had realized that we didn't just want Jezebel. We wanted *Tampon Run* to be even bigger. As long as we were doing this thing, we might as well try to make it as big as we could. Normally the idea of reaching out to strangers and asking for help seemed pushy and scary, but I felt indescribably driven to spread the word about *Tampon Run*. In addition to continuing to push myself to speak up and share my ideas, I aspired to help people feel more comfortable talking about periods.

After creating the game, all I could talk about with everyone was my period. It was amazing to let myself talk about a subject that I had felt so closed off to for seventeen years, and I had to share that feeling with everyone.

So, late on September 3, the night before the first day of my senior year of high school, I sat at my desk wearing my oversize polar-bear pajamas from fifth grade and posted the link to tamponrun.com on Reddit. I'd heard of another simple Web game, *Kanye Zone*, that had gone viral there. Next I went to BuzzFeed (because that's where I always read about viral things) and saw that users could create their own posts for the "BuzzFeed Community," so I did that. I also emailed the link to a few speakers and to our Girls Who Code teacher, Sean, then created Facebook and Twitter accounts for *Tampon Run*. We planned to send the game to people with big networks, with the hope they'd help us get the word out. Neither of us used social media much. We both had Facebook accounts, I used my Instagram occasionally, and neither of us had ever touched Twitter, but we figured that to go viral we needed to use social media, because that's how these things seemed to work. I stared at our empty Facebook and Twitter pages, zero likes and zero followers. It was a sorry sight. Part of me felt so dumb for even setting up these accounts because, realistically, I knew that no one was going to see them other than our friends and family. Like winning the lottery or getting free dessert at a restaurant, I assumed that going viral happened to other people but not to me. I was just a normal person and normal people had to be up to get ready for the first day of senior year of high school in seven hours. I sat for a moment longer, imagining myself looking back on these accounts a year or two later. Future Sophie would probably laugh at their emptiness. But at least we were trying.

"Check it out!" I chatted Andy with the Reddit link. "And have a great first day at school!"

And then, just when I was about to close the computer and call it a night, I received a "SOPHIE" in response. "Change the spelling of 'embarrassing' in the second slide," Andy wrote. Whoops. Spelling had never been my forte.

"Okay, sorry, changed it," I wrote her ten minutes later. And then a minute later I sent, "Wait I spelled it wrong again." And then, again from me, "Wait no that was right. I have a lot of spelling issues."

I refreshed the Reddit link one last time (maybe it was more like four or five times). Objectively it wasn't doing very well, but the four upvotes (which is sort of like the Reddit version of a Facebook like that bumps the post to the top of the page) and three comments seemed BIG to me. Someone had posted their high score (398! That was 127

more than mine!) and two others were debating whether
people should discuss periods at the dinner table. I couldn't
believe that there were strangers somewhere out there sitting at their computers with *Tampon Run* and the menstrual
taboo on their minds. We were accomplishing what we set
out to do, albeit on a very small, seven-person scale. Still,
I was amazed.

"There's a mini debate going! Like a three-comment
debate, but still," I chatted Andy. "Should we respond to
them?"

"No, let's just let it flow," she advised. For a second time
her chat stopped me just as I was about to close my computer.
"YOOO SEAN POSTED IT. YOOOOOOOO." Sean had
posted the *Tampon Run* link to the Girls Who Code Facebook
group, which every GWC graduate from every program
across the country is a part of. "Yay!" I wrote. "I'm so tired,
I'm gonna go to sleep. It's been an exciting night. G'night."

I shut my computer and laid out my clothes for the next
morning: my Hawaiian shirt (of course), a black skirt, my
beat-up Adidas sneakers (another staple), and my camera. We
had completed stage one of releasing *Tampon Run*, but really
my mind was more focused on the day—and school year—to
come. I didn't want to go back to late nights writing essays,
back to the pressures of excelling as much as everyone around
me, and crying in bathroom stalls about 89s and 93s. Up
until this point in high school, I had measured my self-worth

by how well I did in classes, and my main source of learning, growing, and challenging myself was through my school-work. And now that senior year was beginning, I couldn't stop obsessing over what lay beyond the next twelve months: college.

That night I spent hours awake in the dark, obsessing over what the future would bring. What would it feel like to step back inside my high school building tomorrow? To sit behind a table in a classroom with a notebook in front of me? To feel that awful pit in my stomach every time a teacher posed a question to the class? I hoped that what I had learned at Girls Who Code would stay with me at school, but the environment there was so different that I wondered if it would. I wanted to cling to whatever summer I had left, to my last moments of uninterrupted joy before the school year began. But at some point in the darkness I finally gave up and fell asleep.

The next morning I woke up to a chat from Andy that she had sent at one thirty a.m.: "SOPHIE IT'S DOING SO WELL. GWC peeps are posting and sharing and it's beautiful. I love it. Also violence is misspelled on slide four." As I mentioned, spelling is not my forte.

"Whaattttt," I replied. Then I refreshed the Reddit link. While the page loaded I fantasized that we had thousands of upvotes. In my mind the small, three-comment debate from last night had transformed into a long, full-blown argument. Next I'd check Twitter and everyone from President Obama to the Dalai Lama would have already shared the game. Soon the whole world would be abuzz with discussion about the menstrual taboo. It would be 2014: Year of the Period. But when it finally loaded, I found we only had forty upvotes and the debate over the link had died down. Well, so much for *Tampon Run* going viral on Reddit. We had no new notifications on Twitter and the only new email in my inbox was from Walgreens alerting me "40% off Posters + Enlargements." At least the Girls Who Code community liked the game. I moved on to the larger problems at hand, like getting dressed and eating and going to school. I put on my Hawaiian shirt, clammy hands struggling with the buttons, ate some oatmeal while reading the *New York Times*, the mush sticking to my dry throat, and then walked to the subway with absolutely zero inkling of the insanity to come.

ANDY

The first day was normal. I went to classes, talked with my friends, ate lunch, met with teachers, had volleyball practice . . . nothing unusual happened. And I didn't expect anything to. But as I was getting a ride home from my dad, my phone buzzed. A text from Sophie. Hm.

"LOOK WHAT MY MOM JUST SENT ME! AHHH," Sophie texted me, punting an article from *Metro* UK my way. I'm sorry. What?!? *Metro* UK? Could it be possible that *Tampon Run* reached the United Kingdom? How could the journalist have found *Tampon Run*? It had only been— I checked my watch—maybe seventeen hours since we published *Tampon Run*. There was no way someone could have found out about it. From the freaking United Kingdom. But I clicked on the article on my phone, and it wasn't a dud. Someone had written a full-fledged piece on our game—and we hadn't even asked them to!

"WOOAAAHHH!" I responded to Sophie's text. "WOW THIS IS SO COOOOOOL."

"THERE ARE OTHERS TOO. WOW AHH WOW AHH WOW." Caps were in no shortage that night.

I sat at home on my bed, reading the *Metro* article over and over again. "Periods aren't really a great source of lols but this could be about to change thanks to Andy and Sophie (that's all we know)." *That's all we know.* I laughed. We had slogged over the game and spent tons of time putting together a list of outlets to reach out to—but we had forgotten to put anything on the site other than the game and my pixel art representation of us with our first names. We didn't think to add our last names, bios, and contact information, since we didn't anticipate that anyone other than our friends and family would actually find and care about *Tampon Run*. We were figuring it out as we went, which meant we were inevitably going to make some mistakes along the way. All the author of the article knew about us was our first names and that I imagined myself in a Chewbacca costume and Sophie imagined herself in a bathrobe and tiara. That night Sophie jotted down bios and contact information, and I immediately added the copy to the site.

created by: andy & sophie

We also made a *Tampon Run* email account, and the emails started out pretty infrequent, cute, and fangirly. Sophie and I would respond to them with "Thanks!" and "So glad you liked the game!" But by the end of the day, and for weeks after, our inbox was full of emails—and not just fan emails, press requests! Sophie and I became a blur of choreographed email drafts and responses. We were constantly texting each other, and Sophie would often alert me that the notifications on our Twitter account were doubling and tripling. We were answering interview questions, responding to emails, and scheduling phone calls and in-person meetings nonstop. The messages were so positive, like "tamponrun.com has changed my life for the better. #tamponrun" or "Way to go, girls! As a girl who has coded for over 10 years now I love seeing how so many girls are getting inspired lately . . . we do need more powerful girls around :)."

Texts between me and Sophie –

9/4, 11:26 p.m.
Sophie Houser
this has been such a crazy night

9/4, 11:26 p.m.
Andrea Gonzales
i know

9/4, 11:26 p.m.
Sophie Houser
wow

9/4, 11:26 p.m.
Andrea Gonzales
**i keep reading my responses to messages out loud
and kate is like SHUT UP**

9/4, 11:26 p.m.
Sophie Houser
**hahahaha
I keep doin that too!**

9/4, 11:27 p.m.
Andrea Gonzales
and like there was a moment when i was just like
hopping around the room and like dancing
and flipping out

9/4, 11:27 p.m.
Sophie Houser
hahahahaha
I've just been hunched over my computer and then
sometimes i break out into laughter
i feel insane

9/4, 11:27 p.m.
Andrea Gonzales
HAHAHAHAHHA
i like thumped my chest a couple of times
i just dont know how to cope with this yet

9/4, 11:28 p.m.
Sophie Houser
poopiepoopiepoopiepoopiepoopiepoopiepoopie

9/4, 11:31 p.m.
Andrea Gonzales
im going crazy

9/4, 11:32 p.m.
Sophie Houser
hahaha
me tew

It took a while for me to believe that I was responding to real people who had real reactions to *Tampon Run*. They were excited about a game, excited about talking to us! We just felt like normal girls—we'd heard about viral stars, but never in a million years did we expect to become that. We were struck by the power of code. We had started from nothing, created something . . . and now it was making a lasting impact on the environment we lived in. We were average teenagers! Who knew nothing about social media or marketing! We were barely able to set up our own website and get the game online! But now? *Tampon Run* was reaching strangers around the world. It spread like wildfire, thanks to social media and the internet. Never would I have ever expected anyone to share something that Sophie and I made, or at least, not without us begging them to. It was a testament to how profoundly *Tampon Run* had impacted, and could impact, other people. And Sophie and I felt incredibly honored to be the bearers of its very important message.

-10-

LETTING THE WORLD KNOW:
WE <3 OUR PERIODS

SOPHIE

Overnight our lives changed completely. In between classes and during free periods and after school, Andy and I were doing interviews over the phone or typing out answers over email or responding to tweets and other messages of support. My friends endearingly called me "email girl" because I walked around school with my laptop open to my inbox in one hand and my backpack in the other. Andy and I got the same questions over and over: "How did you come up with the idea?" and "What personal experience with the menstrual taboo have you had?" and "What was it like learning to code this summer?" Journalists were interested in writing about *Tampon Run* because our story was a positive one about two young women making noise in the tech world, where females were a minority, and about breaking down the menstrual taboo. The press wanted to capture and package that positivity for the masses. Still, we were amazed that people around the world were struck by and curious about our little project. The menstrual taboo was a very real issue that no one had been addressing, and now *Tampon Run* was giving people the opportunity to talk about it.

I had set out to learn to code the previous year because I hoped to find my voice and achieve greatness and make a positive impact on people. Now, it seemed like somehow, suddenly, on a small scale, my fantasy was actually coming true. I had used coding to make something, and people beyond my family or my friends or my teachers were finding it and enjoying it.

Soon we had been written up online by *Time*, *Seventeen*, CBS, and many other places, and we'd been mentioned on *Conan* and *Late Night with Seth Meyers*. Suddenly I could (and did) Google "Tampon Run" or even "Sophie Houser" and pages and pages of press links would pop up. It felt unreal. Again, this type of thing was not supposed to happen to me. But while all the press felt like a dedicated person's elaborate prank, the feedback we got from users over email and Twitter felt very real. These responses were the most fulfilling part of the *Tampon Run* experience. Some were funny menstruation stories, some were questions on how to start coding, some were encouraging Andy and me to stay in the tech industry. Some were short and some were long. Knowing that real people all over the world had played my tiny summer project and it had moved them enough to send me an email or tweet, that was real. I couldn't believe I had the power to build something that could resonate the world over. I couldn't believe I had taken a chance and pushed myself by releasing *Tampon Run*, and instead of being ridiculed or told my idea was dumb, I was being told over and over again that someone liked it, that someone was moved by it. I felt suddenly full of purpose. I had done something that had helped and changed others. My ideas mattered to someone other than the pages of my journal. There were strangers out there who valued my voice.

Not only strangers reached out to us about the game; our friends and acquaintances did too. One guy friend from school told me that *Tampon Run* made him recognize how weird it was that he felt so uncomfortable about periods. Other guy friends talked openly with my girlfriends and me about our periods, something that never happened before the game. Once, a female classmate I had never spoken to told me randomly that she was going home early because her period cramps were so bad. It was nice, but also, why had this person, basically a stranger, decided to share her period troubles with me? I wasn't just "email girl," I was "period girl" too.

I couldn't stop thinking about that brief but intimate conversation during my walk to the train that afternoon. I loved that she had felt comfortable enough to casually talk about her period to me. But it also made me wonder how my acquaintances and friends viewed me. In my mind, *Tampon Run* was a small part of myself, a recent development, but I was still the same person. I still loved to write and take photos and hang out and do nothing with my friends. I was still shy. On one hand it felt cool to be known for speaking up about something I was passionate about. But on the other hand I was scared to be defined so publicly by *Tampon Run*. While I cared deeply about breaking down the menstrual taboo, it wasn't the only issue I cared about and I wasn't interested in committing myself to that issue and nothing else forever.

I was also scared to be defined by *Tampon Run* because that's not who I really was. Tampon Run Sophie was confident, loud, strong, unafraid. Real Person Sophie still got uncomfortable in new situations, still asked her mom for advice on everything, still got nervous up on stages, and still got scared of speaking up even about the little things. Just because I had put *Tampon Run* online and everything had changed overnight didn't mean that my whole personality had too. I felt like there was a pressure to live up to an image of someone I wanted to be, and hoped to one day be, but that

I wasn't. It seemed like I would be caught any day and my ruse would be up.

The *Tampon Run* response had changed me in some ways, though: it made me see my schoolwork in a new light. I had done something that was touching and helping other people around the world; I felt fulfilled. Whereas my schoolwork, even when I got good grades, made me feel trapped in a tiny, isolated bubble. What was the payoff for an A on a paper? I wasn't helping anyone other than myself by writing an essay or completing a problem set. I was used to measuring my smarts by how well I did in school. Now I was finding that I didn't need grades to measure my self-worth. I could get good at something else—in this case, coding—and measure the quality of my ideas by how much they helped others. I was beginning to see that there was so much more out there than the little bubble that was high school and that I didn't need grades to measure my success. Instead I could define my success through the impact my passions and my creative projects had on others.

ANDY

While most of the feedback on *Tampon Run* was wonderfully supportive and enthusiastic, we did get a handful of negative comments about the game in chat rooms and via Twitter;

some gamers complained that it was too easy to play (they clearly missed the point), and a few people said they preferred not to discuss bodily functions publicly. But these comments never prepared us for the interview with radio host Jay Thomas, which put us directly in his line of fire and really threw us. Jay Thomas is an actor and comedian who appeared in TV series like *Mork & Mindy*, *Cheers*, *Murphy Brown*, and on *Late Night with David Letterman*. Since 2005, Jay has hosted *The Jay Thomas Show* on SiriusXM. If we had done our homework about him, we might not have said yes to this radio interview, or at least we would have shown up better prepared. But since we were keen to shout about *Tampon Run* from every possible rooftop, we said yes to almost all press requests and had no idea what we were in for when we entered the Sirius building that fall day.

As Cristina, our contact and the producer at *The Jay Thomas Show*, navigated us across the floor, we were surrounded by other recording booths. We heard snippets from all sorts of hosts: pop DJs, talk show hosts, sports announcers, news broadcasters. Cristina led us into one of the booths and instructed us to sit on high chairs and put on headphones. She then pointed to the mics that we each had to use, saying, "We're going to go on air in just a second. You can hear Jay finishing up the last section. Get ready!"

We listened to Jay Thomas booming in our headphones, oozing confidence. "And now I have two young ladies who created a video game called *Tampon Run*! I wanna hear all about this."

Sophie and I gave our spiel. Cristina and the sound engineer would chime in on the radio, helping to keep the conversation going. And as we were talking about the hypersexualization of women in video games, the rest of the conversation unfolded something like this (though we don't have access to the official transcript of the interview): "What about Beyoncé?"

". . . What about her?" We laughed nervously. That was not a question we'd been asked before.

"She's all over the place, barely wearing any clothing, shaking her tush everywhere. She's super sexualized, and she does it deliberately. Why do we celebrate that?"

"I think it's because she does it deliberately," Sophie started.

"YEAH," I blurted. "When she claims her own sexuality, she's empowering herself and taking ownership of her body. On the other hand, female video game characters are mainly designed and developed by men—taking the power away from women."

"What about Kanye?" Jay pressed.

". . . What about him?" I was growing nervous.

"You said you liked his music." (I did.) "He, among other rappers, can be incredibly womanizing and antifeminist . . . How do you reconcile that?"

I didn't really have an answer. Weakly, I responded, "I think there's something to appreciating the art that he makes—the production—and not the message that he carries."

Cristina voiced her approval, and so did the sound engineer. The conversation then turned to a Facebook post about vagina cupcakes and whether we would eat them or not. I responded of course. They're cupcakes!

I thought we'd escaped the worst, until Jay moved on to our future projects. He asked something along the lines of "Is there going to be a *Tampon Run II*?"

"Hahahaha, not at the moment," Sophie said. "We're really caught up with *Tampon Run* right now, but we wouldn't say no to working on another project together in the future—"

Jay suddenly laughed. "*Condom Fight!*"

What?

"*Condom Fight*—like, a battle game where you fight to

make a hole in the condom, and impregnate the woman!"

WHAT?

Jay howled with laughter.

"Um . . . no?" Sophie said, smiling awkwardly with disbelief. "I don't think that's a good idea."

Was he serious? Who did this Jay guy think he was, anyway? White, male, and entitled, apparently. I frowned.

"Yeah, I don't think we'd ever make that." I glanced at Cristina and the sound engineer, who seemed to be embarrassed, laughing nervously.

"THAT'S ALL THE TIME WE HAVE! Nice talking to you girls!" Jay boomed, and suddenly it was over. He had moved on to another topic, and we were back in the hallway with Cristina.

Sophie and I were silent. What just happened??

We said good-bye to everyone in the room and fled the building. As we walked back out into Times Square, I couldn't wrap my head around the interview. I was exhausted, first of all. We had sprinted straight from a talk at Sophie's high school that day to the Sirius building. But most of all, I was outraged by Jay Thomas's behavior. Who was he to think that a condom game was appropriate? Condoms aren't even related to menstruation—the only thing that condoms and tampons have in common is that they both can go in a vagina! The more I thought about it, the more irate I became. I thought it was totally uncalled for, totally irrelevant, and absolutely shocking that a middle-aged man would suggest that two seventeen-year-old girls make a game about impregnating women. I was also upset that neither of us had been prepared to field the questions he threw at us. It's like when you get in an argument with someone, and only think about the good comebacks you could have made after the conversation is over.

The fact is, not everyone is going to like you on your way to the top, and Sophie and I had to confront that. As we headed to the subway after our visit to SiriusXM, I was reminded of an article Nikki had sent me when we released *Tampon Run*. We had launched the game in the midst of the crazy online movement Gamergate. Gamergate began when female developer Zoë Quinn released a text-based video game called *Depression Quest*. Her ex-boyfriend Eron Gjoni made the claim that Quinn had cheated on him with five other men, some of whom were in games or game journalism. The internet's conclusion: Quinn had most definitely slept with these men to publicize her game (which was not true—according to Quinn, of the five men Gjoni named, there was just one journalist she'd dated, and he only once briefly mentioned her in an article *before* they dated!). Quinn's phone number, email, even her home address were made public by internet trolls and harassers, and the barrage of hate mail was so intense that she had to flee her house, fearing for her safety. Gamergate advocates quickly moved on to other women in the gaming community, like developer Brianna Wu and critic Anita Sarkeesian, also forcing them to leave their homes because of the sheer number of graphic rape and death threats they received. These Gamergate advocates hid behind the veil of "ethics in video game journalism," but they ultimately boiled down to a small yet very loud group of cyberbullies.

The tech world has so much to offer women, men, and everyone else, but before the day the industry treats us all equally, it will always have a dark side. And, until then, I would just have to muscle my lady self through.

A few blocks from Sirius, Sophie and I came across M&M World. It's a candy lover's delight; giant M&M signs spun up the building, and tourists walked in and out with the trademark yellow M&M World bags.

Sophie turned to me. "Andy, I think we should go check it out."

"YES," I answered, and we walked around the store, eating M&Ms together, laughing at the random novelty items and enjoying each other's company. It was a bittersweet day.

WE OUTTIE TO SILICON VALLEY

ANDY

Months later, *Tampon Run* was growing and growing, with no end in sight. It had completely taken over our lives! We were thrilled! We were talking to lots of people about the experience, and whenever we talked to adults, they always asked us one big question: Was *Tampon Run* IT? What were Sophie and I going to do next? Would we be game designers for the rest of our lives?

I guess that's technically three questions. But they all pointed to our future—and that scared me. People expected that, because of the success *Tampon Run* had, I was all done. My future was set. I liked games, I made a game, and the game did well, so I *must* have found my "thing." Everyone seemed to have figured out my future for me . . . but I wasn't sure I'd figured it out for myself.

Then, in early October, we received an email that was like the universe saying, "Andy, go forth and figure it out." The email was offering us an opportunity to get a closer look at the tech industry; it was an invitation to fly us out to California. The email was from Joe Brown, one of the software engineers at Weeby.co, a gaming start-up in the famous Silicon Valley, an hour south of San Francisco and home to Google, Facebook, and many other leading tech companies. Joe and his coworkers loved our *Tampon Run* story and our efforts to encourage more females to code. Weeby.co wanted us to visit their offices, familiarize ourselves with their gaming technology, and then use their tech to develop a game at a game jam they were cohosting with the Stanford Alumni Association.

If you're not familiar, a game jam is an event where two or more developers team up to design, plan, and build a video game within a specified period of time while competing against other teams. It's just one type of developer gathering, or "hackathon." Hackathons can be as short as a few hours and as long as a few days. They are targeted toward college students and happen in universities all over the world, all the time. They are like sporting events for developers. And there's a whole culture and community around hackathons, just like with sports. If you're going to be a computer scientist, you are definitely going to come across a hackathon—and it is definitely worth being good at them.

At this particular game jam, we would be competing for sponsorship from large mobile development firms. These firms would offer their resources and advice to maximize the winning game's reach. With that kind of sponsorship, we would be able to work on a new project, launch it in the App Store, and get a much wider impact than if we released it ourselves. It was a huge opportunity and had the potential to really grow the "Sophie and Andy" brand. And we couldn't believe we were being offered the opportunity to travel to the epicenter of the tech world and experience it from the inside!

There was just one thing standing in our way: convincing my parents to let me go. At first, the problem seemed to be they thought I'd miss school. But then Weeby.co was kind enough to book us red-eye flights so I could make it back on Monday in time for class. So I discovered the actual problem was that I had never flown anywhere without my parents before. They had only ever let me travel alone for highly structured events with school, like a few days in Baltimore with my robotics team. They didn't even like it when my sisters or I slept over at friends' houses. To them, I was still a little girl who wasn't ready to take care of herself. But there was no denying what the hackathon would give me in terms of insight into the industry and networking opportunities, and I took full advantage of that to convince them. And after multiple conversations about Opportunities and My Future, I got them to agree. Still, it was on one condition: that a grown-up chaperone us. We all decided it should be Cheryl, a film producer, director, and the founder of her own production company, Creative Breed. Also Sophie's mom. When *Tampon Run* went viral, she stepped in as our de facto manager, giving us guidance and insights into handling the press and opportunities that *Tampon Run* suddenly offered us.

So, on a rainy Wednesday in late October, my dad dropped Sophie, Cheryl, and me off at Newark Airport. We unloaded our bags, and then I gave my dad a big hug.

"Thanks for letting me do this, Dad," I said. I really meant it. I knew how much trust they were putting in me. Essentially, this was a "business trip." It was an amazing opportunity, and even though they knew that, it was hard to see their daughter jump on a plane and fly across the country for a few days, surrounded by people they hadn't met and didn't know. If it weren't for my dad's computer programming job, or his interest in video games, I never would have been interested in computer science in the first place. And as much pressure as they put on me, they were also an endless source of encouragement—without that, I may not have been motivated enough to prepare myself for a career in CS. In some ways, it felt like my dad was passing me the torch: I had inherited his love of video games, and now I was going to California to share my love of gaming with others.

Hours later, as the plane crawled away from the terminal, getting ready to take off for San Francisco, I popped a Starburst in my mouth—*This one's for you*, I laughed to myself, sending a silent shout-out to my family at home. Whenever we fly, my parents buy me Starburst to chew on to keep my ears from popping. It felt weird doing the trip alone, foreign and unusual. I wasn't wrestling with my sisters for armrest space. My mom wasn't asleep next to me, and my dad wasn't flipping through the assortment of available movies and TV shows the plane offered.

After the plane's ascent, the seat-belt light dinged off. "So . . . the food." Cheryl pulled out a large bag. "I have lots of leftover roasted vegetables, nuts, apples, and a few kinds of cheese."

I looked at Sophie, bewildered, but she acted like this was the most normal thing in the world. My family never packed leftovers or whole blocks of cheese for a flight.

"Mmm yaaaaaas," Sophie said, reaching for some cheese from her mom. It wasn't just a slice, but a solid block of mozzarella. Sophie tore off a piece for herself, then offered the block to me. "Have some!"

I took the proffered cheese, eyeing it cautiously before breaking off some for myself. Sophie seemed totally unfazed by the small feast Cheryl had brought, and it struck me how different my family was from hers. This California trip was the first time I would see Sophie and Cheryl interact over a long period of time. I basically sat in on their lives during the few days we spent together. Seeing how different their family interactions were from ours made me reflect more on the relationship I had with my own parents. I couldn't believe how openly Sophie shared everything going on in her life with her mom, and how Cheryl shared everything about her life just as openly with Sophie. Whereas with my parents, they were both very hands-on, and also very hands-off. Even though we all loved each other deeply, we kept to ourselves, telling each other only what was necessary. And all the while they remained very protective and controlling.

To some extent, it had to do with my academic work. If I did unusually poorly on a test, in the scheme of the semester it was something I could recover from. But since I worried that they would crack down on me if I made a small mistake, I'd just give them my report card at the end of the term instead of opening up to them about getting a bad test grade and how it made me feel. It happened with my social life, too. When I went to concerts, movies, hung out with friends (particularly guy friends, and alone)—they easily found ways to become nervous or worried about my well-being. I constantly had to gauge what to say, when to say it, and how much information I should divulge. I knew they worried because a bad grade or a bad reputation could affect my future, but I liked to handle things myself. They were overprotective and yet they loved me so much—it took a lot for them to let me go, and I appreciated that. I was growing up, and away from them, and we all had to come to terms with it.

As we neared California, I became increasingly anxious about the experience Sophie and I were about to have. We would spend the weekend interacting with seasoned, successful game designers, venture capitalists, and Stanford alumni. And we had never really coded competitively before. It seemed very possible that Sophie and I would both bomb this and embarrass ourselves. My biggest fear was that Weeby.co would regret spending all the money to fly us out there, finding themselves disappointed by our lack of programming know-how and by the game we would create with their tech tools at the game jam.

The next day, we headed off to the Weeby.co office to meet with Joe. I was surprised to learn that Joe was taking a break from school (in his case, college) to work at Weeby.co. I realized this taking-time-off-from-school phenomenon was a thing in the start-up world. In Joe's case, he seemed so swept up in working at Weeby.co that I wondered if he would ever go back to get his degree. He was particularly excited about the educational potential of their technology. Weeby.co's mission is to make building games easier, simpler, and more accessible, while also offering complex features like leaderboards, power-ups, and social integration with Facebook, Game Center, and other social sites. Their hope is that by providing easy-to-use tools, even coding novices can learn quickly and build their own games.

Sophie and I wanted to drive public discussion about another issue plaguing girls and women, just as we had with *Tampon Run*. We brainstormed around problems we had

personally encountered that we could highlight and sati-
rize through the gaming platform. Ultimately we decided
to tackle the issue of catcalling. It resonated with both of
us—having grown up in New York City, we were often
prey to catcallers wherever we went, regardless of what we
were doing or wearing. And for a while, I even thought
catcalling was normal. Catcalling made me feel unsafe,
unhappy, and disrespected, and I assumed it was up to me
to protect myself. I knew I should walk on streets with
people present, with lots of light, and with my headphones
turned off. And I had picked up tricks to make myself feel
safer at night: pretend to be on the phone, walk faster, quietly grab my pen in case I needed to jab an attacker. But it's
not normal or okay for anyone to be catcalled! I shouldn't
have to be the one making myself feel safe from catcallers!
It wasn't about me changing how I dealt with catcalling; it
was about teaching others that catcalling was bad to begin
with.

Before the game jam, we'd been allowed to hash out the
concept and features of our game, but we couldn't actually
program anything until the competition started. We talked
through our concept for the game with Joe, who would be
helping us with the coding during the hackathon as we got
used to Weeby.co's technology. We all decided it should be
structured like *Tampon Run*, and we even named it *CatCall
Run*. Catcallers would approach the girl and, to fight them

off, instead of throwing tampons, she would throw tools of education like pencils, books, and calculators, and the catcallers would be able to "graduate" once they had been "educated."

Sophie, Joe, and I were all excited about the concept, though as we traveled to the game jam location, Sophie and I were daunted by the thought of actually bringing *CatCall Run* to life. We would have only twenty-seven hours to build the new game—and we wouldn't be able to use any of our code from *Tampon Run*. Even if we were, the Weeby.co technology we were going to use was so different it wouldn't have been helpful anyway. Once the twenty-seven hours were up, everyone competing would demonstrate their games to a panel of judges of leading venture capitalists, game company executives, and Stanford alumni. The game jam took place inside the office of StartX, a start-up itself that's a nonprofit start-up accelerator (an organization that provides budding start-ups mentorship and funding), in an office building in Palo Alto, the same town as Stanford University.

Joe set up his MacBook and his monitors at one of the desks, and so did we. At exactly noon on Saturday, the competition started. Everyone around us launched into action with a constant whir of developers running between computers, team members, and an endless supply of food. Joe set up the initial framework for our catcall game, walking us through the Weeby.co tech. Slowly but surely, Sophie and I picked up on it, executing our own coding processes as Joe either confirmed that our approach was right or explained how we were doing it wrong. We were coding in JavaScript, but using an entirely different code library—it felt strange to use the new technology, similar to learning a new language. But we quickly got the hang of it, working nonstop and watching the hours melt away as we scrambled to build a game in the twenty-seven hour deadline.

Even though the game jam was a competition, everyone was so enthusiastic and eager to share their work. They were also supportive and encouraging of me and Sophie, since we were such an anomaly there. While I was impressed with the caliber and range of the games being built, I was less impressed with the gender and racial diversity in the room. There were very few women and even fewer minorities, which is something that needs to change.

By the time night fell, we needed a break, so we walked around the hackathon and talked to other teams about the games they were building. While I thought I would be shy and tongue-tied, I was surprised by how comfortable and at home I felt there.

We had the thrill of meeting an extremely accomplished and brilliant woman, Laura Deming, an acquaintance of Joe's and the third person in two days I met in the Bay Area start-up world who had dropped out of school to work in the tech arena. I was shocked to learn that she started working at a lab at UC San Francisco when she was only twelve, attended MIT when she was fourteen, then dropped out to accept a $100,000 Thiel Fellowship, a grant for students to drop out of school to launch a start-up or pursue research. Now Laura, at age twenty-one, was a partner at the Longevity Fund, a venture firm focused on funding companies and research that targeted how to reduce or reverse the effects of aging. I was struck by how confident Laura seemed in both herself and what she was doing. But what fascinated me the most about Laura was that she'd completely disregarded any conventional path to success, and still came out on top. She took whatever path she wanted, and was motivated enough to find her calling and follow her passion. To be honest, I was in awe of her—she was so smart, so powerful, so successful— and I wondered if I could be in the same position when I was her age. I was impressed by how much she had already accomplished and by how she had remained so down-to-earth and relatable—to the point where, when she asked us what we most hoped to get out of our trip to California, I didn't hesitate to jokingly reply, "I want to try an In-N-Out Burger!"

From there, the hours ticked on . . . ten . . . eleven . . . midnight . . . Sophie and I began to lose steam. We were almost twelve hours into the jam when Joe looked up from his phone and turned to us.

"Hey, guys . . . Laura left you In-N-Out downstair—"

"NO WAY!" I exclaimed. Sophie burst into laughter. We couldn't believe that this busy, important person had taken the time and gone to the trouble of bringing us In-N-Out burgers. She was nice, too! It was moments like this when I was sure I was exactly where I was supposed to be in life.

By two a.m., after fourteen hours of working, Sophie and I hit a wall. Weeby.co had booked hotel rooms for us in case we needed to sleep in beds, but we were so entrenched in our work we didn't want to leave, even for a little bit. Part of the hackathon culture is that you code through the night, sometimes for days on end, without any sleep. Very few people seemed to be sleeping—instead, they mulled around the snack table, hunched over their computers, and chugged Red Bull and coffee as they powered through the night, running on fumes to get their games done. We were determined to make the best game we could, too—using ALL the hours allotted—so, bleary-eyed, Sophie and I agreed to take shifts resting while the other one continued to work on the game. It was the start of Daylight Saving that night, so we did two o'clock in the morning twice. Some of the extra-ambitious programmers seized the additional hour to do another hackathon online—so, a hackathon within a hackathon—where they scrambled to make some semblance of another video game during sixty minutes. I was impressed with their

stamina and zeal. I certainly was in no condition to do a hackathon within a hackathon. At around five a.m. I hit my limit and fell asleep under a desk for an hour while Sophie continued our work.

We were relieved that by late morning on Sunday, *CatCall Run* was taking shape. Now at least we would have something to show the judges and other teams when we had to reveal our game later that afternoon. For our main character, we pulled the Luna art from *Tampon Run*, but changed the color of her dress. I made her from a bird's-eye-view perspective and then Joe coded her into the game for the times when she ran. We created pencils and calculators and a Start screen for the game. Slowly but surely, all the pieces of programming that we worked on finally joined together for our finished game.

Promptly at three p.m., we rushed downstairs to set up our demo for the judges. For about half an hour, they circled the tables of games, scribbling notes on their clipboards. Given the other teams' incredibly impressive games, Sophie and I were shocked when we were announced as finalists. We were excited and honored, but now had to scramble to prepare a pitch to present to the panel of judges and other leading tech-world people gathered in the room.

When we walked on stage fifteen minutes later, we were hit with a striking realization: All but one of the panelists were men, all much older than us, and all big shots in the professional mobile game industry. It was overwhelming for a number of reasons. Every time we introduced *Tampon Run*, there was this fear in my head that everyone would completely reject it, and I wouldn't know how to respond to that. In California, we were introducing *CatCall Run* to a whole slew of people, most of whom were men who had probably never experienced catcalling themselves. Plus, it was the first time we had written a presentation with so little prep—up until this point, we had carefully plotted out and planned every one of our speeches. But while our presentation-on-the-fly, delivered in a sleep-deprived state, was not our best public speaking moment, the audience and judges boomed with applause when we were done. We certainly had piqued the judges' interest, and they weren't afraid to ask us questions: How were we going to monetize the app? Why was fighting catcalling important to us? But it didn't seem interrogative, it seemed exploratory, like we had the opportunity to educate the judges on something that they didn't necessarily think about regularly. We were introducing an entirely different perspective to them, and *CatCall Run* gave them the opportunity to discuss it—an opportunity that they wouldn't have had without the game.

I felt so proud of us! We had held our own at a hackathon competing with professional game designers, and we had gotten a taste of the start-up world of Silicon Valley. Joe had helped us code and adapt to the Weeby.co technology, but it was the concept behind the game—a concept Sophie and I, two high school girls, developed—that the judges and audience responded to so enthusiastically. We had taken on another major social issue. That was no cakewalk. We expanded our horizons, met new people, and added to our networks. Venture capitalists, entrepreneurs, and professional game designers eagerly approached us throughout the hackathon, genuinely interested in us and in exploring ways they might work with us in the future: Did we plan to launch a girl gaming company? What other projects were we working on? Were we open to collaborating with others? It all felt totally surreal—but by the end of our trip, I think California left me with more questions than answers.

I wasn't sure if I wanted to continue to compete at hackathons, which are a big part of the culture if you major in computer science. Hackathons are exhausting, and I still don't know how I feel about programming competitively. And while many people in the start-up world were encouraging us to start a girl gaming company, being a start-up founder, at least from my perspective of that weekend, didn't seem so appealing either. Running a start-up is a huge undertaking: founders and employees work extreme hours, often sacrificing any life outside of work and shouldering extraordinary responsibilities. And launching a company would mean taking tremendous risks that I wasn't sure I was ready for. If my start-up failed, I would hold all the accountability: I'd have to answer to my investors, lay off my employees, live with the embarrassment of failing, and have to start all over again. Of course a degree and expertise in computer science can lead to many paths other than competing in hackathons and launching a start-up, but coming out of that weekend, it was difficult to see beyond the two most obvious routes. So the realization that hackathons and start-ups might not be for me was scary. I wondered where I could fit into this industry if not here. And if I didn't fit into one of these categories, what would I do?

– 12 –

SACRIFICE CITY:
WE DEAL WITH THE TOUGH STUFF

SOPHIE

When Andy and I got back to New York after our whirlwind California trip, I began to see that life post–*Tampon Run* was as intense as it was rewarding. The game was helping create positive social change, making me understand the incredible power of technology, and pushing me out of my comfort zones, but it was also time-consuming, overwhelming, and stressful. All these frustrations and feelings came to a head one day when I found myself crying uncontrollably in the girls' bathroom at school. I had arrived ten minutes late, tired and hungry, after staying up till all hours to finish every last bit of homework—and the sight of my first-period classroom had cued the sobs. I was crying real, fast, overwhelming, I-can't-get-words-out-because-I'm-crying-too-hard tears. It all felt like too much. While I was happy *Tampon Run* had turned into something major, I was having a hard time juggling it with seeing my friends and performing well in all my classes. So here I was: bathroom, feelings, tears.

All of a sudden I was struck with a moment of great clarity: Sophie, oh my God *what*? You're in the bathroom crying over *grades*? Why are you still so obsessed with doing schoolwork and getting perfect grades? I loved the satisfaction of hearing a lecture or finishing a book and learning something new, but getting good grades had nothing to do with learning and everything to do with proving I wasn't worthless. I had already received affirmation from the outside world for *Tampon Run*. I had proved I was smart and ambitious and creative. Did getting an A on a paper or a 98 on a math exam really matter? School wasn't the ultimate judge of my intellect. Not to mention that successes outside the classroom were rewarding in a new and exciting way, and could actually have a positive impact on people, which felt even better than acing a test. Yet here I was, holding on to this school-obsessed aspect of my old self. And as much as I felt like the world and my parents expected me to get good grades, I knew that need actually came from within me. I had always set the bar high and saw anything other than perfection, especially in school, as failure. If I was going to stop caring so much about my grades, then it had to be my choice to let go. And I knew full well that out there in the world beyond high school, what people valued was different. No one at the game jam had asked to see my transcript before they let me in. The panel of judges didn't want to know what I got on my last history test. All they cared about was that I had good ideas, worked hard, and was passionate.

So I tried to let go. Of the stress and anxiety over my grades. Of the obsession with being first at everything. I stopped crying over good-but-not-great test scores. I stopped staying up until all hours to finish every small homework assignment. I asked for extensions when I needed them. And over the course of the fall, I tried putting nonschool stuff higher on my priority list, too: doing activities that made me happy in the moment, doing nothing with my friends, biking around the city, and writing in my journal. Activities that made me feel blissful and giggly and like the side of me that I loved being: the comfortable, fun, carefree side.

I wanted to be great, and *Tampon Run* had provided a small taste of greatness—as well as the workload and stress that come with it. I had known before *Tampon Run* how important the blissful nothing moments of life were to me, but I was now realizing that having the free time to do whatever was crucial to my happiness. While *Tampon Run* had been hugely fulfilling and fun, it also was pushing me into uncomfortable situations constantly. Places where I was forced to speak up for myself, voice my opinions about coding and the menstrual taboo, and constantly meet new people. On the other hand, activities like hanging out with my friends were comfortable and easy. Instead of feeling like I had to live up to the *Tampon Run* version of myself—the confident, savvy, unafraid Sophie—I could just be myself. I could be scared and silly and unsure. I missed that level of constant comfort that I felt with my friends. But I knew that "being great" required sacrifices and required investing myself in my work. I don't think Voldemort had a lot of time to just hang out and pursue his hobbies on Friday afternoons. So how could I fulfill my dreams of both being great and being a normal person? Or would I have to choose in life between the two?

ANDY

I really, really, really loved to keep myself busy. Aside from the mountains of work lovingly bestowed on me by school, I found myself signing up for tons of extracurricular activities. ECs were a way for me to socialize, make friends, and learn outside the classroom. From September to December, I'd be on the volleyball team. From January to April, I'd spend time at my robotics team's workshop in Midtown. I also half-assedly managed boys' volleyball, filling the rest of my time preparing for piano evaluations and spring choir concerts, or stage managing for the play festival. I'd always been able to handle it all, but once *Tampon Run* happened, everything spilled over.

For a while, answering press inquiries between classes was fun. Running around the city for interviews was fun. Taking phone calls, going to photo shoots . . . I loved all of it. It was so unusual, so far removed from anything I could have imagined. I didn't mind missing a volleyball practice to get to an interview. I knew I could postpone hanging out with friends to work with Sophie. I could miss a homework assignment because I could make it up tomorrow. Putting aside the "normal" stuff was fine, since this was a once-in-a-lifetime experience.

And for a while, it felt right. It felt GOOD.

Until it didn't.

At Hunter, Spirit Day is the Best Day of the Year. The entire school piles into buses and drives up to Bear Mountain. We spend the day there, and a lot of people watch the junior-senior flag football game. Between *Tampon Run* stuff and my extracurriculars, I managed to squeeze in a few practices with the junior girls' football team. I was lined up to be a wide receiver, and I couldn't have been more excited. But Spirit Day conflicted with our California trip—I had to choose *Tampon Run* over high school. So on Spirit Day, I wasn't scoring touchdowns with my friends; I was on a plane touching down in California. As excited as I was to go to the hackathon in Silicon Valley, I was devastated to miss Spirit Day. All my friends were having a once-in-a-lifetime experience . . . and so was I, but not the one I'd expected.

After California, I began eyeing *Tampon Run* in a more skeptical light. Before I knew it, it was the end of the volleyball season, and I had barely gone to practices, much less played in games. I had no time to study for the SATs, which were suddenly only weeks away. My schoolwork faltered, and every bubble of free time I had was filled with phone calls, emails, or interviews.

But despite a million different things begging for my time and attention, someone liked me enough to believe I had the time for romance too . . . so he asked me out. And I said yes.

Let's call him Nate. Nate was awesome—smart, athletic, pretty dorky, and really attractive. We always wanted to be around each other and to talk to each other. We cared about each other immensely, and despite how busy we both were, we were determined to make it work.

But spending time with Nate was near impossible. Our schedules seldom lined up, so we took advantage of free periods during school and brief breaks in our day. Time alone with Nate also meant less time spent with other people in my life. And on top of it all, I had to keep our relationship a secret—my parents thought dating was solely for the purpose of getting married and having kids. They worried I'd be called a slut, or somehow be deemed lesser because I was involved with someone. They thought boys would be a bad influence on me, and I would get distracted from the "more important things" like school, and grades, and college. So the act of just having a boyfriend added significantly more stress. But I loved this guy, so why not?

Regardless of what was going on, I still felt compelled to prioritize *Tampon Run*. I was determined to make the game a success, and I didn't want to let Sophie down by calling it quits. I felt like all of the opportunities *Tampon Run* gave me were incomparable, and I shouldn't turn any of them down. And each opportunity was fleeting—I had to take advantage of them while they were still available, whereas Nate and my friends and extracurriculars would always be there. The game felt like a wave had crashed over me months ago, but only after the trip to California did I realize I was drowning.

What suffered most was my piano. I've mentioned this before: I grew up studying, living, and breathing piano. So as a freshman I signed up for the Young Artists Program, a stand-alone program for high schoolers who wanted to continue studying piano intensely . . . maybe even to apply to musical conservatories for college. For the two years I was in the program before *Tampon Run*, everything went pretty well. I no longer had the time to practice as much as I did in elementary school, but it was incredibly rewarding. Then *Tampon Run* pushed piano further and further to the back of my mind and it became totally neglected. But unlike a lot of my other activities, piano wasn't something you could cram for. Preparing pieces can take months of intense discipline. By the end of the year, I barely had one piece ready. In the end, I didn't just do badly on the program's final performance—I failed. I was disheartened to see how music, which had been such a crucial part of my life, was suddenly shoved into the corner like an old toy. I knew I wasn't going to become a professional pianist, but I thought piano would always be a priority in my life. By the end of my junior year, I felt like it had completely disappeared from under me.

I questioned why I was putting everything aside for *Tampon Run*. I loved working on it and I loved seeing my work have a positive impact on the world around me. *Tampon Run* was so rewarding and so fulfilling. But I wasn't prepared for the sacrifices I would have to make to do the work I loved. Every instance where I agreed to do something for *Tampon Run*, I was shaving off time I could have devoted to something else: robotics, volleyball, friends, a boyfriend, family. I wanted to commit to everything, because I really enjoyed everything.

But, in my heart, I knew prioritizing *Tampon Run* was all my choice. I could have stopped working on it, denied all the press requests and phone calls, and kept doing my other extracurricular activities. But I didn't. *Tampon Run* and piano were two big parts of my life, and one of them had to give. Even though I felt like piano was slipping away, and that sucked, the reality is that I was letting it go. If this was what it meant to grow up—to let go of things I loved—then I wasn't sure I liked growing up. I had chosen to make *Tampon Run* a priority and to invest myself in it, and it brought me immeasurable happiness, but like most things in life, the whole picture wasn't black and white.

13

A PIVOTAL MOMENT AT PIVOTAL LABS

ANDY

Fast-forward two months, and Sophie and I were exploring the next stage in *Tampon Run*'s expansion: mobile apps.

Fast-forward two months, and I still wasn't sure what I was going to do with my life. Grown-ups were still asking the same questions about my future, and I was still giving the same unsatisfactory answer: "Hahaha, maybe! [Making a game company/working on another project with Sophie] sounds super fun! We'll see what happens." But I wasn't sure what I was expecting to happen, what sign I was looking for. I felt uncertain, embarrassed, and a little afraid, when I should have felt excited, assured, and confident. When it

came to *Tampon Run*, Sophie and I focused on the present—
we barely had time for what was going on now, much less what
was going to happen. Then we met Nihal Mehta, Reshma
Saujani's husband and a successful venture capitalist (someone
who invests in start-ups) who specializes in mobile apps.

During the winter of 2014, Nihal pushed us to take the
next step with *Tampon Run* and make it a mobile app. We
hadn't been planning on it, but now it was clearly the next
move for us. A mobile *Tampon Run* app would give us a
much wider audience than just the Web game. Phones have
overtaken computers as people's main source of sharing and
receiving information. We looked at the data from our *Tampon Run* website, and a significant number of visitors were
going to the site from their mobile devices or tablets. But
neither Sophie nor I had ever done mobile development,
except for one week at Girls Who Code. We knew that
making a successful mobile app would require a lot more
resources, time, effort, and knowledge. And far more sophis-
ticated coding than we could have mastered at the time. So
Nihal eagerly e-introduced us to someone at Pivotal Labs,
one of the world's leading companies that develops websites
and apps. Pivotal works with amazing places like Twitter,
Refinery29, and Groupon. We were excited to get advice
on developing mobile applications from this well-known,
accomplished development firm.

So, following an invitation from Pivotal, there Sophie and

I were, anxiously waiting in their reception area. We decided
to stand while we waited for someone to come usher us into
our meeting. At Girls Who Code, one of our speakers said
that we should never sit while waiting for an interview.
Standing puts you on the same physical level as your interviewer when you first meet him or her, and you wouldn't
have to spend those few awkward moments gathering your
belongings as you stood up. While we paced back and forth
across the reception area, Catherine, the manager of the New
York office (there are Pivotal Labs offices around the globe),
came out to meet us. She ushered us into an enormous white
and gray cafeteria. It consisted of their kitchen, eating, and
lounge space with what seemed like a huge supermarket for
millennials. The lounge space was a vast room full of sofas,
TVs, musical instruments, Ping-Pong/foosball tables, and a
massive spread of food. The supermarket covered an entire
wall—two-thirds of it was fancy refrigerated beverages,
fancy yogurts, fancy fruits, and other classy foods, and the
other third was drawers upon drawers of granola bars, chips,
candy, and so much more. Sophie and I had seen a number of
office kitchens on our *Tampon Run* adventures, but this one
blew all the others out of the water.

"Take whatever you like! In the mornings, there's free breakfast before the daily meeting. So if you are ever able to come that early, you're welcome to have some."

Sophie turned to look at me, perplexed. *Ever able to come in the mornings?* What did she mean by that? I shrugged, launching myself at the Boylan's root beer in one of the fridges and snatching a bag of Dirty's potato chips.

After Sophie grabbed a coconut water and Siggi's yogurt, Catherine led us across the lobby and through another set of glass doors. We found ourselves in a huge white room with gray carpets and a ton of desks. People were scattered across the open office layout, talking to each other, drawing on giant notepads and Post-its. Some people were working at standing desks, some people sat down, and of course, everyone had food. There were so many people! At least, a lot more people than I expected. We were then led to a conference room where three other employees, Linda, Sam, and Alex, were prepped with notepads, Post-its, Sharpies, and pens.

"Have a seat!" Catherine instructed us. "We have a few questions before we get started in the next few weeks."

I glanced at Sophie. What the hell was going on here? She looked back at me equally confused and with a twinge of panic. Neither of us knew what was going on, but everyone else was going along with it. Cheryl was supposed to join us for the meeting, but she was running late, so we were forced to fend for ourselves in her absence. But neither of us was prepared to do so.

The four Pivots (the term for Pivotal employees) began to rattle off a series of questions:

"What demographic are you looking for?"

"Are you trying to make revenue?"

"How much do you prioritize different platform development? iOS? Android? Both?"

They put up giant Post-its, scribbling on them. Their line of questioning was very specific—I thought we were going to be asking them questions, for their advice? I looked at Sophie and Cheryl, who had arrived in the middle of all the questions. They both had the same perplexed looks on their faces.

"We're just wondering what this is all about?" Sophie said. "We're really excited for where this seems to be going . . . but we're just a little confused."

Catherine smiled. "Totally valid. It's just a seven-week contract, and you'll have a team of two full-time developers,

Sam and Alex, and a designer, Linda, working with you."

The three of us were silent. . . . What?

"You're going to work with us? On the app?" I stuttered. This was more than we could have ever dreamed of.

"It would be an honor to have Pivotal work with us on the mobile app, but we support *Tampon Run* on our own," Sophie said. "It's our money. And I know Pivotal is very expensive to hire. . . ."

"We'd like to do this pro bono," Catherine offered. "There are far too few women in tech and Pivotal wants to support you as young women in the field. Our gender distribution in general is pretty good, but when it comes to programmers, we're really lacking. A lot of our female Pivots work as designers and project managers. We really hope to help make a difference, and we really love your game—we're so glad we get to work with you!"

We were stunned. Catherine explained that we would pair with Sam and Alex every day after school to program the mobile version of the game and Linda would help us with the artwork and designs. In disbelief, we couldn't stop saying thank you.

It was incredible that such a large tech company cared about fixing the gender imbalance of their employees enough to work with us for free. Pivotal isn't the only company committed to addressing the gender gap in the field. In January 2015, Intel announced that it would invest $300 million dollars to help close the gap. Google and Twitter are also spending huge sums to support the tech education and recruiting of females. And major funders of Girls Who Code like Google, Facebook, and Twitter have pledged to hire Girls Who Code alums to increase their female tech employees. Although the gender imbalance in the industry is a major problem, it's also one that most tech companies recognize and are trying to address. Pivotal's offer made the tech industry seem less like a Big Evil Thing that's trying to stop me from succeeding—instead, it helped me understand that we're not the only ones who recognize the issue. A lot of people are working to fix it, and if I work in tech, I'd be able to find resources and a supportive community.

For us personally, Pivotal's help with the mobile app was huge. Sophie and I barely knew where to start when it came to developing a mobile app, and now thanks to Pivotal, *Tampon Run* would be accessible to anyone with an iPhone in seven weeks. And we'd get to learn mobile development along the way.

Every day after school, I'd book it from Hunter to Pivotal, grab a San Pellegrino and potato chips from the kitchen, and sit down with either Sam or Alex to work on code for the evening. After an entire day at school, Sophie and I were totally drained, and learning and understanding the code required a lot of focus, since the work we did at Pivotal was so over our heads. We both had coding foundations, but now we were suddenly coding an app from scratch. On multiple occasions, I found myself falling asleep, and so did Sophie, and then we'd quietly nudge each other awake. But it was never out of boredom. We were so excited to be there, and loved pairing with professional coders. Alex, Sam, and Linda were incredibly patient with us, as we stumbled our way through Objective-C (one of the languages used to program for iOS devices).

Throughout our seven weeks at Pivotal, Sophie and I got an eye-opening, front-row view of what it's like to work at a highly creative, well-run tech company. I especially loved the open and collaborative environment among its employees, fostered partly through daily office stand-ups where everyone stands in a circle after breakfast and anyone can talk about the work that they're doing or any announcements they have. At the end, everyone claps, signaling the end of the morning meeting and the start of the workday. The morning company-wide stand-up ensures that even though it's a big place, everyone has a sense of what everyone else is doing and feels part of a community, a shared experience.

Collaboration is also central to the way the Pivotal coders work. All coders pair program, meaning two developers share one computer: one person does the physical typing, while the other person talks through the code that they're supposed to type and the thought process behind it. This is practically unheard of in the tech world, where normally each coder is seen as too valuable to have two coders working together on the same thing. However, Pivotal's mantra is that while pairing might mean that coders write fewer lines of code each day, the quality of the code they write is better. Pair programming means that coding is a constant conversation. Each programmer is always checking the other to see if there are holes in their logic or errors in their code.

Sam and Alex told us that during their first few months there, they were exhausted at the end of each day from pairing. But they grew to love it. They get to interact with someone all day, have conversations, and create high-quality code. I also had a hard time with pair programming at first. As I've mentioned, I'm the type who struggles to ask questions, brooding over a problem for way too long before asking for help, so I found it difficult to be forced to talk about my problems or confusions while I paired with Sam or Alex. But by the end of the seven weeks I discovered that talking through the code with a partner allowed that person to poke holes in my ideas and helped me understand the pros and cons of the way I was approaching my code. It was also invaluable to learn to communicate my ideas and problems to another person.

Pivotal seemed like an incredible place to work and, since I was going there every day after school, it was starting to feel a bit like a job, a really, really fun and comfortable job. I had imagined that my life as a programmer would be a lot more isolated than it was at Pivotal. Aside from meetings, I thought that I would have my own desk and write my own code. I thought I would be working on the same, or similar, projects most of the time. But working as a programmer at Pivotal was nothing like that. The paired programming made the job more social than most others. The programmers worked in small teams directly with their clients, which meant they were constantly contributing ideas to the final product. And since their projects changed all the time, they never got bored. Pivotal's practices weren't the norm in the tech world. By working at Pivotal and seeing how they equally prioritized work and their employees' personal lives, I knew it was possible to lead a balanced, sane, fun existence as a coder. I had sometimes worried that the life my parents wanted for me might not align with the life I wanted for myself, but now that I could imagine being a coder at Pivotal, it seemed great. And my parents loved Pivotal—they knew I was exhausted from commuting to school and Pivotal and back home, but they also knew how much *Tampon Run* meant to me and how much I could learn there. To them, I was happy and I was working toward a career we had set out for me, both of which were true.

During our seven weeks, Sophie learned that she got into Brown University, so I thought about (and talked a lot about) my future during those weeks. Alex heartily recommended that I go to a school that I could afford. "The amount of debt for college is never worth it," he said, which seemed like excellent advice. The financial burden of college always hung over my family's head—or at least, mine. Of course my sisters and I would want to go to the best colleges we could get admitted to, but in reality, we'd have to consider the amount of aid we'd be given. I assumed I'd go to the college that gave me the best financial aid package—and because programmers are desperately needed in the world, you can pretty much get a job anywhere, regardless of where you get your CS degree, as long as you're good. Sam and Alex even talked about my future after college, excitedly planning my career as a computer programmer.

"You can come and intern for Pivotal!" Sam told me.

"And when you're done interning, you can work here!" Alex finished. Maybe I would!

At the end of the seven weeks, Sophie and I had completed the *Tampon Run* iOS app, new and improved from the simpler Web game we had initially created. We had added a new enemy, new graphics, and the game now got harder as the player engaged with it. It was a beauty. The night of February 2, the day we released the app, Sophie and I weren't together. We exchanged a couple of texts throughout the day and checked in with Pivotal to make sure everything was ready. Then I got a text from Sophie.

"Pressing Submit now. I'm really excited!"

"Me too!" I answered, my heart jumping.

I was psyched about the release of our updated game, and was also proud that I had just spent the past two months going to work every day at one of the top tech companies in the world. It was mentally stimulating and interesting, *and* I still had the opportunities to talk to a lot of people. But beyond that, Pivotal started to answer the questions California left unanswered about how I could find my future in tech. As obvious as it seems, it turned out there wasn't just that one path—the high-pressure and fast-paced hackathon and start-up scene—I could take to be a successful programmer. There was another type of programmer life, the one I'd tasted at Pivotal, that might be the one for me . . . if I decided to be a programmer at all.

WHO RUN THE WORLD?
(GIRLS!)

SOPHIE

All the events I attended throughout that first year bolstered my aspirations of being great and making a mark on the world, and using coding to do that. Like Laura Arrillaga-Andreessen had said, I wanted my time on this planet to matter. But as I talked to more and more start-up founders, it hit me that I didn't aspire to become a coder. I wasn't interested in coding someone else's ideas my whole life or being part of a huge company's engineering team. I dreamed of coming up with my own ideas and then, with my coding skills, having the power to build them myself. I hoped to launch my own start-up one day. I wasn't sure what problem it would solve or what field it would be in, but pursuing coding meant that I could tackle anything in any field. After all, entire industries are being overhauled thanks to technology: how movies are distributed (e.g., Netflix), how people book "hotel rooms" when they travel (e.g., Airbnb), and how people get around (e.g., Uber).

So, by the spring, I sought more than just casual run-ins with company founders. I decided to use my network to hear from them firsthand about what it was like day-to-day to manage and build a start-up, how they got the ideas for and launched their companies, the biggest challenges and fears they faced, and how they juggled the huge demands of launching a company while living their lives. I was especially interested in meeting female founders, because I was eager to hear about their experiences in the tech world. There are not only far too few female coders in tech, there are also far fewer female start-up founders than male. In 2012, remarkably only 5 percent of tech start-ups were owned by women.

I started working up the guts to reach out to founders and ask if we could grab coffee. It still took a lot of self-coaxing to set up the meetings, and then I'd always arrive feeling young and tiny on the inside. But, as I had learned to do, I projected poise, confidence, and happiness on the outside. I stood up straight, went over my memorized questions, and walked with purpose. I wondered, of all the confident people I met every day, how many of them were constantly panicking on the inside too? Probably more than I thought.

Despite initial nerves, I walked out of every single one of these meetings feeling energized and inspired. My meeting with Sarah Adler, the cofounder and chief technology officer (CTO) of Spoon University, made me think about what I might major in in college. If I dreamed of having an impact on the world through coding, I assumed I had to hone my coding skills in college and major in computer science. So I was surprised to discover that Sarah had majored in journalism. She didn't even learn to code until after she had graduated from college and took classes at General Assembly, an organization that offers training in a range of tech-related skills. Later, I learned that programs like General Assembly are becoming increasingly common as more and more college graduates decide they want to learn to code. It's incredible that Sarah didn't get into tech until after college, given that she's responsible for building and maintaining the technology at Spoon U, which enables students at any university to create a Spoon U offshoot for their school, with the support and community of the central brand. Sarah was the first person to open my eyes to the possibility that I didn't have to major in computer science to fulfill my entrepreneurial dreams. Maybe knowing some code was enough. Which was good news, since I also loved reading and writing and philosophy and history, and I wasn't ready to close myself off to those things just yet. But I have to admit, once I got to college six months later, I saw the possible value of majoring in computer science. The starting salary of a coder can be around $100,000 per year (!), and coding is one of the few jobs that have more positions than qualified people to fill the roles. The US Department of Labor predicts that in 2020 there will be 1.4 million computing jobs but only enough qualified college grads to fill 29 percent of those jobs. So if I majored in CS, then I could hone my coding skills more deeply at a time when I don't have to worry about supporting myself too. And since I know I want to work in tech and start-ups, it's crucial to have these skills even for summer internships and after I graduate. To major in CS or not to major in CS: not an easy decision!

Over coffee with Sarah, we also discussed her experience as a female entrepreneur. "I don't really like being seen as a female entrepreneur," she said right off the bat. Yes, she was a female entrepreneur, yes, she was a female CTO, yes, she was a woman who coded, but why did "female" need to come before all of those other identities? I mulled over this question as I walked through Midtown back to the subway. I had never thought about that before. I had entered the tech world as a "girl who codes," so my gender had always been central to my identity here. But should it be? What's the difference between a "girl who codes" and a "person who codes"? Part of me felt, since there's such a gender disparity in the field, I should be shouting from the rooftops that I'm a female and that I'm here, doing what relatively few girls and women are doing. But I understood Sarah's point too. I shouldn't be defined by my gender. I didn't want to be noticed or special because I'm a female; I wanted to be noticed and special because of my skills and my intellect and my personality. But because there are so few women in tech, being labeled as a "female coder" or a "female founder" is inevitable. Until there are more women in the field, my gender makes me different.

Miki Agrawal is another (female) founder who is getting noticed in a big way thanks to her smarts and guts and creativity, and also because she's taking a strong stance on a women's issue close to my heart: menstruation. Miki cofounded Thinx, underwear for women who are having their periods. In 2015, the company tried to put up eye-catching ads—photos of pink grapefruits that looked like vulvas—with the caption "Underwear for women with periods." New

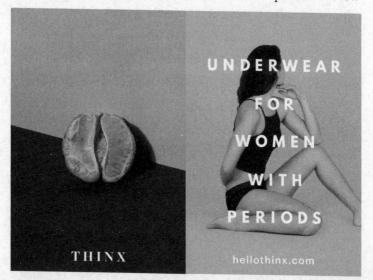

York's Metropolitan Transit Authority, the agency that runs the city's subway system, claimed the ads were inappropriate, despite putting other much more explicit advertising in subways, like ads for breast augmentation.

The incident serves as another example of the menstrual taboo: that a positive ad about menstruation and the female body was deemed inappropriate, while another that encourages women to fit into unrealistic societal norms about their body is totally fine. Miki didn't take no for an answer and after an uproar over social media and lots of press about the incident, the MTA let the ads run. Miki was (and is) a strong role model of the type of founder I'd like to be. She's gutsy and she channeled her own desire for an alternative to pads and tampons to create a successful product. I also admired her generosity and commitment to social good. For every pair of underwear someone buys, the company donates money to AFRIpads, which trains women in Uganda to sew washable cloth pads and sell them at affordable prices.

Miki was also a role model in how she seemed to maintain a social life despite working around the clock. I love my friends, hanging out, and being social, so I wanted to determine how you launch a company without sacrificing that. I saw Miki enjoying social time when I went to the Thinx relaunch party at Miki's restaurant in Williamsburg. Yes, I'm not sure how, but in addition to starting her own company, she also opened a restaurant and wrote a best-selling book.

The restaurant is beautiful and was filled with other young entrepreneurs and incredibly tasty gluten-free pizza. It seems that Miki has found a way to merge her passions for food and feminism with entrepreneurship and fun times, often intermingling them all. It's exactly what I wanted.

Another (female) founder I learned a lot from is Liz Wessel, founder of WayUp, a job site for college students looking for part-time work, internships, and entry-level positions. I not only had a coffee with her, I got to observe her in action all summer as an intern at WayUp. She had just raised $7.8 million dollars for her company when I met her, and the company had just graduated from the most prestigious incubator in Silicon Valley, Y Combinator. Y Combinator invests in a select group of start-ups, gets others to invest too, and invites all the start-ups to Silicon Valley for three months to train them.

On a hot July day—nearly a year since I first set foot inside Girls Who Code—I approached the WayUp office wondering what they would assign me to do. What if I didn't know how to do something? What if I messed up? What if I wasn't dressed correctly? I had subbed out the Hawaiian shirt for one with a more toned-down floral pattern. It seemed more adult, more "job-y." I was especially nervous because this internship was my first taste of working at a real company. I had worked at an art gallery and a physics lab before, where my assignments were contained and simple. But I knew that start-ups were tumultuous and fast-paced. I had no idea what to expect.

Spending all day inside was a huge adjustment. I hated watching the sun glide through the sky outside the small window without ever touching my skin. I'd check Snapchat and see my friends running around the city, enjoying our last summer together before we all scattered for college. Meanwhile I ended each day exhausted from having to be "on" for eight hours straight and handling the types of social interactions where you have to be confident and attentive for every second. Everyone around the office was nice, but I couldn't be myself. I couldn't be loud or weird or crack jokes. It felt like I was dealing with another small-scale *Tampon Run*. This was work and none of the people in the office were my friends. I had told myself that I aspired to be Liz, that I wanted to work at a start-up that summer, that I wanted to work hard in an internship. But that first week I worried that I didn't actually want any of those things, I only wanted to want them. I was dying to hang out with my friends in the park all day, to enjoy the things that made me happy in the moment rather than feeling uncomfortable, just so Future Sophie could be happy.

But in the second week, everything changed. I discovered that I *could* be myself at the office and that my job allowed me to tap into my passions. One morning during my second week, my boss, Nina, who had graduated from college only a few years before (as had just about everyone at the company), told me they needed promotional images for WayUp campus reps to share on social media. The reps are college students who spread the word about WayUp on their campuses and get other students to sign up and use the site.

"Familiarize yourself with the images we have right now and then create some of your own," she told me. And that was it. The rest was up to me. When I got assignments in school, the teachers usually provided a clear framework for how I should do them. I know how to write an essay. I know how to do a math problem set. But this was completely different. I was being given free rein, which should have been exciting and liberating but instead was paralyzing. What if what I delivered to them was bad? What would they say?

I sat at my desk staring at the clock. Nine a.m. turned to ten a.m. turned to eleven a.m. Girls Who Code had taught me that the only way to accomplish something overwhelming was to start doing something, anything. All I could do, I decided, was to make what I found funny and take it from there. Making strange Photoshop scenes (friends' heads on weird bodies, weird birthday cards) was one of my favorite pastimes anyway, so this was just turning a pastime into a job. Isn't that the dream?

Whenever Andy and I were photographed for *Tampon Run* we were asked to "look normal" while we fake coded or to "laugh normally." I'd pull up Google images of pizzas for us to scroll through to make us laugh. So for Andy's birthday I Photoshopped a pizza-themed version of *Tampon Run* with the Jolly Green Giant—the emblem of vegetables—as the enemy. Then I folded up a printout and stuck it in a cardboard tampon applicator.

I ended up spending the rest of the day cracking myself up while perfecting my Photoshop skills and blasting music through my headphones. What if cats used WayUp? So I Photoshopped that. Or what about babies? So I Photoshopped that too. What if all the Teletubbies had the WayUp home screen on their stomach televisions? So I made that happen too. I lost track of the sun moving through the sky outside, lost track of the clock on the wall, lost track of the fact that I was at a job.

"Wow, you're so good at Photoshop," my boss said when she looked at my creations. "These are hilarious." I was an

amateur Photoshop enthusiast who had spent the last six hours just having fun and now I was being told I had done something good. Maybe work wasn't so bad. My Photoshop creations were as "me" as I could get and my boss had liked them. Maybe I could let myself be me even in a job, even at WayUp. Just because something was called a "job" didn't mean that the work had to be meaningless and lacking personality. Actually, I discovered the more creative and myself I (or anybody) was at work, the better the product.

After the Photoshop success, I let myself be "me" little by little at the office and started having fun when my boss gave me open-ended assignments rather than getting paralyzed by the freedom. One of my tasks at WayUp was writing posts for the company blog. I thought about all the new people Andy and I had met on our *Tampon Run* adventures and how uncomfortable some of those new situations had been. I knew what I would write about: tips for a shy networker. Then I had another idea. This article would be even better if I actually went to a networking event and wrote about the experience. So the next evening I found myself getting off the subway on the Lower East Side to attend a networking event for people interested in social justice.

I arrived at the address of the event site, which was, to my surprise, a bar. I had envisioned an open, airy, pipe-exposed event space, not a dimly lit, packed bar. It started to sink in: I was about to enter a room of people I didn't know without Andy next to me, without even being old enough to be there legally. I backed away slowly, literally, heading toward the corner, back toward the subway. I was having my usual gut reaction: I wanted to be home, safe and comfortable. As I headed toward the subway I called my mom to let her know I would be home earlier than expected. "If you're leaving because you're scared, that's not a good reason. If you're leaving because you're too tired, then that's fair," she told me. I stopped walking. I wasn't tired and she was right.

So there I was, back at the bar, walking in, filling out my name and job on a sticker and scanning the room. What was my job? "High school graduate"? "Full-time student"? "Maker of tampon game"? "Interested in coding"? Those didn't seem like good options. What about "Marketing Team, WayUp"? That sounded legitimate. Okay, so I was only an intern. Okay, so I was only working there for six weeks that summer. But no one had to know that.

I walked through the crowd of adults holding drinks and chatting and I immediately felt young, little, clueless, unsure how to enter any of these conversations. I tried to put on my confident mask like I did before meetings with the entrepreneurs, but I couldn't get it on. So I beelined to safety in the bathroom, where I had a heart-to-heart with myself in the mirror. "You got this," I whispered. I was a *Tampon Run* girl. I had networking chops, damn it! Now watch me ride that tampon. The door of the bathroom swung closed behind me as I headed to the bar and asked for a water. I then promptly made eye contact with a woman standing next to me.

"Hi, I'm Sophie!" I reached out my hand for a shake. I was home free. Our conversation was mediocre, I didn't ask for contact information, but it was exactly what I needed. Talking with her had broken the ice and reminded me that everyone around me was just as clueless and alone and ready to talk as I was. Hours later I left the event proud that I pushed myself to go, pushed myself to talk to people, pushed myself to be a bit uncomfortable and try something new. I thought all I would get out of the night was a good story for the blog, but it ended up showing me I wasn't that shy girl anymore. I had the confidence to step out of my comfort zone and enjoy it. I was very into this new Sophie.

While my friends who spent the summer relaxing were

definitely tanner than me, those months taught me more about the world and about myself than I would have learned hanging out with the same people every day. I got to see what $7.8 million in investment and huge growth actually means: new hires every week, more employees under thirty than over, and a work hard/play hard attitude. I also watched Liz, the founder and a young female founder, in action. She was kind, but firm. She was fun, but she got shit done and expected that from everyone around her. She also exemplified what I had heard from every woman at every coffee meeting: Liz worked around the clock, constantly running from meeting to her email to meeting to her computer.

After my six weeks at WayUp, I felt torn between wanting to be a Liz and wanting balance in my life. I kept coming back to my moment of clarity in the school bathroom after *Tampon Run*. I knew that to achieve anything great you have to make sacrifices and you have to work extremely hard—but at what cost? And at what point does day-to-day happiness, derived from fun with friends and the freedom to take a bike ride or read a book, eclipse the desire to achieve greatness?

The more entrepreneurs I talked to, the more it seemed that the key might be to incorporate the smaller pleasures into my long-term pursuits. Sarah started Spoon University with her best friend from college. Miki combines her passions for feminism and food with her entrepreneurial projects. And Liz created an environment at WayUp where employees worked hard but had a good time and could be creative. Maybe I'd have to sacrifice "doing nothing" for "greatness," but that didn't mean I had to sacrifice a joyful, balanced life to pursue my passions.

– 15 –

THE END AS I KNOW IT

ANDY

In the spring of 2015, DoSomething.org, a not-for-profit organization that empowers young people to create social change, invited Sophie and me to their office to discuss *Tampon Run* and Girls Who Code and to prototype some of their new text-based games about women in STEM. At the end of our second visit, Jon, a mobile technical lead at the company, told us some amazing news—by demonstrating *Tampon Run*'s impact, he was able to get funding from DoSomething.org's board for two summer game-development internships. Our tiny project was affecting the money flow and decisions of a major organization! Equally incredible, Jon wanted the two of us to apply for the jobs. Sophie was already planning to do a nontechnical internship at a start-up (which later became WayUp), but I was super excited about the idea. I had applied for a technology internship at DoSomething a few years ago and didn't get it. I couldn't believe they were now asking me to apply for the upcoming summer! They are an amazing nonprofit—I definitely planned on applying.

If I got the internship, I'd learn even more about coding and I'd be a step closer to a possible career as a programmer. But as I submitted my resume and cover letter, I discovered that I wasn't applying for another high school internship; it was an internship for college students. I was so out of my league. On one hand, I was just over a year away from being a college student myself, but on the other, I felt so much younger and more naïve than one.

"I don't know if I should apply," I told my parents late one night as I got my application materials together.

"Annie, this is a great opportunity!" my dad crowed, using my other nickname. "And if you add this to your resume, think about all the other programming jobs you might be able to get next summer and the summer after that. By the time you graduate college you'll have so much experience that you'll have no problem getting a job! Maybe you could work at Google or Facebook!" My dad might have gotten a little carried away, but he was right. This would be a fantastic opportunity.

A few weeks later I found myself scurrying to find a quiet space to conduct my interview for the DoSomething internship via Skype. Sitting in the corner of my school's auditorium, I was about to have my first-ever technical interview. "Let's start off by going over your code," Jon began. I gulped.

This was gonna be *rough*. A few weeks ago, DoSomething had asked me to solve two problems with code and then send my solutions over before the interview. As usual, I had waited until the last minute to write it, scrambling to submit the code at one a.m. while on a college-visit road trip with my parents. I was afraid my code sucked.

The two assignments had made reference to *Super Mario Bros*. The first part of the assignment was writing code to recognize when Mario ran into a coin, and the second was for when a fireball hits a Goomba (one of the enemies in Mario). When I examined the tasks more closely, they were familiar: two types of collision detection. The Mario and coin assignment was like *Tampon Run*'s rectangle-to-rectangle collision between Luna and the enemies. The fireball and Goomba task was circle-to-circle collision. All I had to do

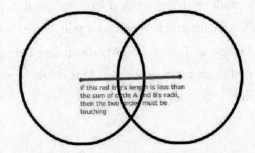

If this red line's length is less than the sum of circle A and B's radii, then the two circles must be touching

was check the distance between the centers of the fireball circle and the Goomba circle. If the distance was less than the sum of their two radii, then they had to be colliding.

Still, the rectangle-to-rectangle collision proved difficult. Even though I had done this type of collision before, the semantics of the instructions tripped me up. They said: "Implement a basic algorithm to determine if Mario has run into a coin."

At first, it seemed just like *Tampon Run*, but I was thrown off by the word "run." *Does that mean Mario is just running forward? Am I not supposed to account for when he jumps or runs the other way?* I had never done a coding assignment for a job interview before; I had no idea if I was supposed to follow the directions exactly, or account for any movement Mario did. I was nervous to do anything wrong because I wanted to get this internship . . . and I didn't want to let my parents down by not getting accepted. Either way I hoped to do my best, so even if I made the wrong choice, I was just following the instructions I'd received.

```java
/* Prompt specifies that Mario has run INTO a coin--not jumped up or down on a coin, or backed up into a coin
 * Only need to identify whether the rightmost face of Mario's collision rectangle collides with a coin
 *
 * @param Coin coin
 * @return whether Mario has collided with a coin
 */
public boolean isHittingCoin(Coin coin) {
    int marioRight = position.getX() + width/2; //gets the x-coordinate of Mario's right side
    int coinLeft = coin.getX() - coin.getWidth()/2; //gets the x-coordinate of a coin's left side

    if (isOnSameLevel(coin) && marioRight >= coinLeft) return true;
    else return false;
    //isOnSameLevel is a function I wrote to check if Mario was at the same height as the coin;
    //If he is at the same height as the coin AND (&&) Mario's right side x-coordinate is greater than
    //the coin's left side x-coordinate, Mario must have passed the coin, and thus, collided with it.
}
```

Jon chuckled, looking over the code. "I appreciate you taking the instructions so literally." I laughed in relief. That could have ended up really badly. "Do you know how to account for other movements that Mario could make?"

"Yes, definitely." I described the logic behind rectangle collision, and Jon nodded along with my explanation. As I kept talking, my confidence grew. I had been so nervous for this interview, but I knew how to code, I was good at this. There was no reason to be nervous.

Just as I was starting to relax, Jon rocked the boat again.

"Right!" Jon stopped to think. "Why don't we do some live coding next?"

"Sure!" I said, pretending to be confident while I was anything but. Live coding, where you're presented with a coding problem and have to solve it in front of an interviewer, is common in interviews for tech jobs. It's a way for the company to watch in real time how a candidate thinks and solves problems. The process is known for being overwhelming and nerve-racking. Live coding was a total wild card: you could either get a really easy problem to breeze through, or else something impossible to solve that could ruin your chances of getting the job. At first, the prospect of coding in front of Jon made me anxious. What if I messed up or I didn't know where to start? As Jon set up the live-coding section, panic set in. This was not going to turn out well, I convinced myself. While I worked myself up, Jon linked me to an online code editor where he could watch and contribute to the code I was writing, sort of like a Google doc for coding.

"So, why don't you make a code version of the game FizzBuzz," he started. "Basically, you're going to write code that counts to . . . fifty. But every time a number is divisible by three, print 'fizz.' Whenever a number is divisible by five, print 'buzz.' But when a number is divisible by three and five, print 'fizzbuzz.' When it's not divisible by either of them, print the number. Sound good?"

I sighed with relief. We had played a verbal version of FizzBuzz at Girls Who Code during our free time; the concept was something I was comfortable with. But I wasn't sure if I could code it easily under pressure.

I took a moment to breathe and decide on a game plan before I shared my thought process aloud. "I guess I'll just start with a for-loop." Jon couldn't see them through the screen, but my hands were shaking. Typing while someone is watching is so much more difficult than you'd think. While I coded, I glanced at Jon. His face didn't hint that anything was right, but it didn't hint anything was wrong either . . . so I kept going.

"Every time we go through the loop, we'll check to see if it's divisible by five and three. If it isn't, we'll check if it's divisible by five and then if it's divisible by three," I said. As I spoke and typed out my code, I felt more and more comfortable. Just talking through my code felt like all the other times I programmed in front of people at Girls Who Code and at Pivotal Labs. I had found pair programming so tedious and difficult back then, but now all that practice was really paying off. I was good at explaining my code, and doing so actually made working through the problem so much easier.

"And if it isn't divisible by any of them," I continued, "it will print the actual number. I think that should do the trick."

I looked up at Jon, nervously awaiting his judgment. "Mmhm," he said. I pressed the Compile button on the page . . . and it ran!

```
1
2
fizz
4
buzz
```

The computer ticked off number after number, and I grinned. "Awesome!"

Jon smiled too. "That's all I needed to test you on . . . I just wanted to make sure you have fundamental coding knowledge. Everything else, you can learn. Do you have any questions for me?"

I didn't have any. I was just relieved.

A few weeks later, they offered me the job. I'd work from

nine thirty to five thirty, and I'd finish their ten-week program just in time for senior year to start. I didn't respond
immediately. Actually, I didn't tell anyone immediately. I
knew it was an incredible opportunity . . . but also a lot of
work, with no time off. I was worried about closing myself
to other opportunities, and I wasn't sure I was ready to spend
my entire summer programming. The real question was:
who would I be doing this internship for? Did I really want
to spend my life as a programmer, or was I pursuing this path
because it's what my parents expected of me? I knew they
ultimately wanted me to be happy, but I also knew that they
had spent their lives making sacrifices so they could ensure
I would have an easier, more financially stable life than
they did. After Pivotal, I knew I'd be happy working as a
programmer—but maybe I'd rather use the summer to
explore my other interests.

What did *I* want? What was *I* passionate about? I loved
piano, volleyball, and theater, but I also loved coding. Partly
just the act of coding, and partly witnessing the impact of
what my code could do. I had witnessed it firsthand with
Tampon Run, which had reached people around the world
and created social good. That had been hugely fulfilling.
Now DoSomething was offering me the opportunity to do
the same thing again. Maybe I didn't know what I was going
to do with my life, maybe I wasn't as sure as my parents that
I would become a programmer, but taking this internship

wasn't locking me into a career path. I would take the job at DoSomething, and I would do it because I wanted to.

When I told my parents I got the internship and was going to accept, they smiled and hugged me and told me how proud they were, and then my mom said something completely unexpected:

"Are you sure? It's a great opportunity, but don't you need more of a break from work?" My dad nodded next to her.

"Thanks," I said, and I meant it. "But I want to do this."

A few months later, at nine thirty on the dot, I sprinted into the lobby of the DoSomething building. Katie, DoSomething's "head of fun," led me into the familiar-looking main office space, a wide, lofty area filled with desks. "Even though you're in high school, you're not a part of the high school program. But a new batch of high school interns will be coming in at ten, so you'll do orientation with them, okay?"

I had known that I was going to be the only high schooler in a program for college students, but now the reality was setting in. The college students had already been here for a few weeks getting acclimated to the environment and starting on their summer projects. I was not only years younger than everyone else, I'd also be running weeks behind the rest of them.

That day I sat down with Jon and Jasmine, a junior at the University of Chicago studying CS. She was the other gaming intern. Jasmine had spent her first few weeks beginning to build a choose-your-own-adventure game about preventing unhealthy relationships. It was text-based, and the user played as a person going to prom. The player has to choose the best language to prevent harmful, rude conversations between the main character's friends.

We sketched out features of the game—the characters, script, and a mini-scenario within the game that I would work on. The mini-game would give me the opportunity to work on video games, collaborate with Jon and Jasmine, and add more interactivity to Jasmine's game. I was super excited. The video game seemed like it could do a lot of good and I couldn't wait to get my hands dirty in coding, and coding for social justice.

The summer flew by. I got used to attending meetings, voicing my thoughts, and engaging with others. I had spent the year learning the importance of speaking up through *Tampon Run*, and now I was getting to put that skill into action daily at work. I loved coding every day—I never had the time to do it during the school year, so designating hours every day toward something I was passionate about made me feel happy and satisfied. But it was also hard. I had the fundamentals down pat, and coding was now certainly easier than doing it for the first time, but I didn't use the same technology I used to make *Tampon Run*. Learning new coding libraries wasn't easy. It forced me to be less afraid of asking questions and not brood over obstacles on my own. When

Sophie and I had worked on our game at Girls Who Code, we emailed each other versions of the code. At DoSomething.org I learned how to use Github, a complicated but useful way to share and combine code. By the end of the summer, Jasmine and I had finished our first iteration of the game. The process turned out to be a lot slower than making *Tampon Run*, but I was proud of how much I had learned.

Although I had been scared to be the only high school student in a college internship, interacting with the older interns turned out to be one of the most valuable parts of the summer. So many of them didn't know what they were going to do. They weren't sure what jobs they were going to have, what majors they were going to graduate with, or whether they were going to graduate at all. They were constantly changing direction. Some of them thought they knew what they planned to be when they went into college and had changed their minds countless times. But no matter what, they were so passionate about what they did. They got to work for a cause they believed in. They were constantly full of ideas and energy, and their drive to make a difference in the world inspired me to do that even more. Whether I ended up pursuing a career path in coding or in something I hadn't even discovered yet, I was sure about doing something that helped others. I knew my parents wanted me to be a programmer, and my summer at DoSomething had solidified my inkling that I, of my own volition, wanted to be a programmer, too. My assumptions about my parents' expectations, however, weren't necessarily accurate. One night that summer, as I obsessed over applying to college and fitting in all my extracurriculars, my mom took me by surprise: "Just do what you want," she said. "And do it well. As long as you visit us, I'll be happy."

Thanks to *Tampon Run*, and everything that came after it, I got to reassess the whole life path I had set for myself.

And I learned to be okay with not knowing. If by next year I discover a new passion and suddenly want to stop programming, want do something else—that would be all right. No matter what I end up doing, computer science will almost definitely be relevant to my work and, like my GWC mentor, Nikki, I could always incorporate my CS knowledge in nontraditional ways. And should the day ever come when I abandon computer science completely, even if I decide to break with the mantra of "doctor, lawyer, or engineer," I know my parents would still love me. And more importantly, I would still love myself.

– 16 –

I FOUND JOY IN A HOPELESS PLACE

SOPHIE

On September 5, 2015, my parents and I packed a rental car with two big suitcases and a lot of Walgreens bags filled with soap and shampoo and paper towels (the little things) and drove off to Providence, Rhode Island, to start my freshman year of college at Brown. I was not only anxious about leaving home and diving into a whole new life, I was also worried about a major speaking engagement in Providence just two weeks away at the Business Innovation Factory Summit, an annual conference where accomplished people tell inspirational stories for an audience of five hundred.

Andy and I had done so much public speaking, I had

learned to accept and control my inevitable nerves by not focusing on the negative (I could lose my voice, forget my lines, or throw up) and instead focusing on the positive (public speaking gave me the opportunity to share something I was passionate about). Still, I couldn't help that my hands got sweaty and my mouth went dry and the blood rushed to my face whenever I thought about getting on a stage in front of people. This talk was also a special situation because I would be solo, without Andy by my side. She was my safety net, and now she would be gone. And I was going to have to talk for a full, long fifteen minutes. A quarter of an hour! Enough time to take a quick nap.

In the days leading up to the speech, as I got acquainted with my new life at Brown (peeing in stalls, living with a roommate, meeting what felt like hundreds of new people a day), I practiced. I practiced first thing in the morning, I practiced as I got lost around campus. I practiced before I went to sleep every night. I told myself I wasn't nervous for the presentation: this was College Sophie, this was Post–*Tampon Run* Sophie. This Sophie didn't get nervous about sharing her ideas in front of large crowds! But telling myself that over and over was not as effective as I'd hoped. The night before the speech, as I began a run-through in front of my dorm-room mirror, I cried and cried and cried and, finally, when I thought I was done crying, I opened my mouth to speak and all that came out was a whimper and more tears.

Just picturing myself giving the speech filled me with stomach pain and lightheadedness.

What was wrong with me? I felt like this was junior
year again, before the speaking circle and the sessions with
Dr. Graham and before *Tampon Run*. I felt like this was my
English class presentation and I was sixteen, back in my
empty bedroom unable to get words out of my mouth and
into the air. I was paralyzed by a fear that I hadn't felt in a
long time, that I thought I had gotten over. "I thought you
changed," my left brain said to my right, which replied, "I'm
sorry. I thought so too."

The next day I stood backstage waiting to go on, clutch-
ing my notecards. I felt physically nervous, sweating and
shaking.

"You're up next. Ready?" someone said.

I nodded, and as I started to put my phone away it buzzed
with an incoming text. It was Andy.

You're gonna KILL the speech today!!! Tell me how it goes!

And you know what, I *was* going to kill it. I had to honor
what we had built and all that we had experienced together
this past year.

And then minutes later I was walking up on stage, clutch-
ing my stack of notecards, and staring out into the dark
audience. I let myself wait a moment before I started to speak.

In the silence I realized that there were just a bunch of people sitting out there watching me. Not one thousand eyes, just five hundred people. Some of them were hungry, some of them were bored, and they all just wanted to hear a good story. And here I was, the 501st person in the room, also "just a person," also a bit hungry, just here to tell a good story. And for the first time on a stage, I didn't feel as if I was being watched and judged like a spectacle. I felt as if I was just standing in a friendly room. I was the youngest speaker of the thirty-two and I was about to tell a great story about my period, about coding, about a tiny game that became so much more—and, damn it, I was going to have some fun. I began to speak, mindfully not too fast, and mindfully not fidgeting, and I reminded myself to focus on the story I was telling rather than the room and the stage and the audience. I could feel the crowd journeying with me. They laughed at all the right places and, up on stage, I took the time to laugh also. It was exhilarating. I felt powerful and relaxed and suddenly I didn't want my fifteen minutes to end.

I walked off the stage shaking, this time in a bouncy, jittery way. I felt incredible and I couldn't stop smiling.

"You were amazing!" my mom exclaimed when I found her outside.

"That felt like a free high!" I whispered. Then my phone buzzed with another text from Andy.

Soph, you must've done great cause we're getting so many Twitter notifications!

I typed back, *Ahhhh that was so fun! I never thought I'd use that word to describe public speaking.*

I spent the next four hours at the after party, eating as much free and tasty food as I could get my hands on. As I floated around with a plate stacked high, people stopped me to say how much they loved my talk, how much I had inspired them. I couldn't believe it. One guy even stuffed a hundred-dollar bill in my hand. "Oh my God, I can't take this," I said, and held it out for him to take back. Was he serious?

"Take it. I'm investing in your future. I know you'll do great things," he insisted.

"Wow, thank you, but I really can't take the money." But he wouldn't take it back.

That night I returned to campus, tired from the day's events and the four hours of networking. I tucked the hundred-dollar bill into a pouch in the back of my desk drawer and reflected on my day. Something in me had changed. Something had clicked on that stage. Wait, no. Nothing had clicked. Huge emotional breakthroughs like that don't just click. That moment on that stage had been the product of a year of stages. And I mean literal ones—at a TEDx event we had participated in, at the Girls Who Code Gala where we'd spoken, at the hackathon when we presented our project—and figurative ones—on the phone with *Time* magazine and in the makeup chair at MSNBC. I had spent a year learning to value my voice and realizing the power it has to impact and move people. I had spent a year being thrust into foreign situations and discovering I had the strength to figure them out. And all of that shone through on stage when I stood there telling my story.

Unlike the other triumphs throughout the year, this one was all my own. I had practiced and prepared almost entirely by myself, without my mom there every moment. I had gotten on stage without Andy and networked without her as my ally. I wouldn't have been able to get through the past year without the help and support of everyone around me: Andy, my mom, the Pivotal team, Sean, Reshma. The list goes on and on. And there were countless more mentors and collaborators who would guide me and push me in the future. But now I knew I also had the ability to make strides on my own. I am my own person. I have the power and I have the capabilities to decide what I want to pursue and what I enjoy, and I don't have to choose just one thing.

And here I was, about to embark on a major personal journey, miles away from my mom or Andy or anything I knew before: four years of college at Brown, where I would be able to study whatever interested me, whatever might help me make that dream of speaking up in big ways a reality, whatever would make me happy.

Aside from all the new classes I took freshman year, I also signed up for computer science both semesters. Just as I had, now and then, resented the amount of time *Tampon Run* consumed, I sometimes resented the amount of time I spent doing CS, holed up in the computer science building trying to solve puzzles with code. Sometimes my code didn't work and I couldn't figure out why and I felt like I was going to scream. It was like getting Luna to jump, but on a daily basis. Nonetheless, coding offers the unbeatable thrill of pressing Enter and watching something come to life on-screen. It offers the unparalleled power that comes with creating something from nothing, all on your own. With code, I have, and anyone has, the power to build a product from scratch, to bring ideas to life, and to reach millions of people instantly. But even if I weren't interested in reaching people globally and moving humanity forward through code, I'd still want to learn how to do it. Coding is empowering, it's creative, and it's fun.

I am determined to spend the next four years acting on my curiosity, trying new things, and not letting my fear of failure hold me back. Because if I don't ever try, then I'll never grow and I'll never learn. And I will never figure out all the different things that could make my life worth living. I don't want to close myself off to any possibility. During freshman year I signed up for a poetry seminar where I had to not only write poems but also share them with the whole class every week. I had never written a poem before. I still get nervous in uncomfortable situations, and that same fear still bubbles up when I try something new. Before I emailed my first poem out to my class, I read it over and over and over again. I sat with the mouse hovering over the Send button and my finger hovering over the mouse, just like I had before sending all those emails to the female founders. My inner voice told me, "You're scared and that's okay"; it told me, "Beneath the fear, you want to press that Send button"; it told me, "What's the worst that could happen?" And then my finger pushed down.

As for Andy and me, no matter what happens in our futures, no matter if we end up going down completely different career paths or if I live thousands of miles away from her, we will always share something special. We've experienced something entirely unique together and we've pushed each other to learn and grow through it. We're forever bonded by sharing the collaborative creation of *Tampon Run*, and the highly unexpected and unanticipated adventures that grew out of it.

Tampon Run set my life on a whole new course. It showed me the importance of just diving in and trying, even if something seems difficult or overwhelming or like you might fail. Because who knows what could happen if you just try? Maybe your simple video game will go viral. Maybe you'll change your life. It also made me realize that I'm capable of achieving something great and that I want to speak up about my passions, no matter how scary that might be. I look back on myself before *Tampon Run*, on that scared junior in high school who had the same ambitions, but was plagued by fear and insecurity and self-doubt. There is a part of me that will always be that girl. I think there's a part of everyone who is that girl. But the people who succeed, whatever that looks like for them, are those who overcome their fears or sense of "can't" and dive into the unknown to learn, to create, to build.

SOME THINGS CURRENT US WOULD TELL PAST US IF WE HAD A TIME MACHINE

✔ Food tastes better when it's free.

✔ You never know what's gonna resonate with people, so don't second-guess yourself.

✔ No one *actually* knows what's going on. So don't be afraid to join in!

✔ Adults are also human.

✔ Parents just ultimately want you to be happy.

✔ Learning to code = being a BOSS.

✔ Sophie is weird lmao —Andy

✔ Andy farts in her sleep! Not even loling —Sophie

✔ Doing something creative and challenging with a friend is so much more fun than doing it alone.

✔ Girl power is real.

✔ Major key to success: collaboration.

✔ JUST TRY. YOU GOT THIS!!

WHERE WE ARE NOW . . .

SOPHIE

In the week leading up to the release of *Girl Code* and our book tour, I found myself (maybe to an obsessive degree) trying to figure out who I'd been fifteen months earlier when I wrote it, who I was in that moment, and how the two were different and similar. It was March and I was a sophomore in college. As the days went by and the book release got closer and closer, I became, almost by necessity, less analytical and obsessive about the "who am I/who was I?" question and excited about the next days of my life. *Girl Code*—something I had created, worked hard on, spent time on—was going to be real for the world to see. Just like with any coding project, we had started with a blank, white screen (in this case, an empty Google Doc). And little by little, through many hours of typing, conceptualizing how to tell my own story, long talks with Andy, and moments of panic, we finally had a full, finished product. We had a book, something we could hold and interact with and pull off shelves.

The day I went to the mail room at school and discovered my own book in my mailbox, I stood there in disbelief. Other students, people I vaguely knew and recognized, walked around me going about their days. To them, I probably looked like I was unwrapping my winter-break read from its packaging. But this book was *mine* and I stood there, beaming joy and amazement into this block of paper. I learned a few minutes later, after sending an excited text to Andy, that she had cried when she got her final copies in the mail. There's nothing like the high and the feeling of power when you create something and can then interact with your creation, whether it's a game you've coded or a book you've written.

Although similar in some ways to creating something with code, creating a book felt different. I once got a call from Sara, our editor, because she wanted to discuss what links we could put in the additional resources section. So I sat down on the nearest bench in the student center and started listing off some resources I could think of. "Okay, that sounds good," she said, and I felt like laughing. Me, eighteen-year-old me, college me, me—*Sophie*, who was sitting in the student center at college in between lunch with friends and class, just said a few things into a phone and now those words were going to be printed thousands of times onto real paper, which would sit in a bundle on a shelf in a bookstore for money. I had always regarded books as some sort of perfect package, made by some *author*, some genius, some expert, some magician. But really, books are just made by people. They are made by *me*s and *you*s who sit behind their computers and write what they feel like writing. And that's true for the whole world. Everything, even the greatest inventions and songs and movies, are the product of some human being doing what feels, sounds, looks, and seems good. "It's funny that I said things and now they're going to be in a real book," I blurted into the phone before Sara could hang up. She laughed a little. "Yea!"

I feel like I should print a T-shirt stamped with the phrase "Books are made by people" because it's one of the biggest takeaways from this whole process. And it's something I began to realize through the *Tampon Run* adventure, too: to a degree, adults also have no idea what's going on. There's no special secret, no magic trick, no something that the author or coder or CEO of a Fortune 500 company knows that I don't. I mean, yes, an author is (supposedly) especially good at writing, a coder especially good at coding, and a CEO especially good at leading—but at their core even the "greatest" are just people figuring it out. And, as with *Tampon Run*, it's simply about putting something into the world that speaks to people and expressing yourself.

Anyways, back to March, specifically March 7, which was a very normal day. I woke up, went to class, and took a computer science midterm (which I learned later I got a 35 on :/ but it all worked out in the end, wooo! I passed the class.). I also posted an Instagram on our brand-spanking-new account (@girlcodethebook) "Happy Pub Day to OURSELVES!!" and that was pretty much it. So in my history, March 7, 2017 is the day I became a published author and it was also a really normal day in my life.

The following ten days, however, were not normal at all. On March 8, I got in a black car with a suitcase (and a dream), said "Peacee outt" to Brown University and my classes and my friends, and sped off into the night. But really I was driven at a normal pace to T. F. Green Airport to embark on

girlcodethebook

Liked by **clemgrace**, **showandtal** and **223 others**

girlcodethebook Happy Pub Day to OURSELVES!! Our book GIRL CODE: Gaming, Going Viral and Getting It Done has hit. the. shelves. Get your copy before they're gone! K thanks, bye!

a ten-day book tour around the country to talk about *Girl
Code* and meet readers (ty HarperCollins!). Our first stop
was Austin, then Tucson, the Bay Area, Providence, Boston,
and finally New York. For ten days, I took a break from
my real life and ate MUCH better food than my school diet
of eggs and canned beans, got driven around in large black
SUVs, stayed in nice hotel rooms—all while hanging out
with Andy. I felt at times like a little kid in an adult's body:
from arriving at hotels and whispering into Andy's ear, "This
is niceeeee," to entering the hotel room and immediately
jumping on the bed.

Although Andy and I have known each other for years
now and have shared something very odd and unique, we've
never spent ten days 24–7 together. As much as this was a
"work" trip, it felt more like an adventure with a very close
friend. A snowstorm on the East Coast left us grounded in
San Francisco for an extra day midway through the trip. We
spent it sleeping late, reading in a coffee shop, and then walking across San Francisco to get dinner. I insisted on walking
on the sunny side of the street and we went, falling in and out
of conversation. Stretches of silence were never uncomfortable (a mark of true friendship) and in the stretches when we
did talk, we covered what only the two of us could understand. What all the *Tampon Run* stuff meant to us, what we
want to do in the future, how we felt about this chapter end-
ing, because as fun and wild as this crazy trip was, it also felt

like the climax to a major section of our lives.

I never planned for any of this: to make it big with my summer project game, to become a figurehead for women in tech and for the menstrual taboo, to write a book about my personal emotional growth. I can't remember my life before all this craziness happened. I have grown up and into this role, and now, after the ten days, it would be over and time to move on. "I'm kind of scared," I told Andy as we (really, me) panted up a hill. The tour had conjured up all kinds of thoughts and questions. *Who am I apart from all of this? Who am I actually? Who would I have been if none of this accidental recognition and opportunity had happened? How can the next thing I do live up to this? And what do I do if I don't even know what I want to do next?* I've been asked, since posting *Tampon Run* online at age seventeen, by reporters, by venture capitalists, by entrepreneurs, by myself, "what's next?" And for so long it's been half acceptable just to say "I'm doing this." But now what? I was scared. I am scared. And then we arrived at dinner where we talked and did not talk and laughed as I chugged tea and ogled the cute baby next to us. When you spend that much time with someone, the move from serious emotional to light nothingness is seamless.

While those ten days stirred up the question of "what next?" they also helped me realize that, while I still don't have an answer, I am well on the path to figuring it out. That's largely thanks to having the opportunity to meet and talk to young people from around the country. We would tell our story (a shortened version of what you just read about), and afterward would answer questions and chat personally with the students. So many of them wanted to learn how to code, but even more exciting was that so many of them had ideas for what they wanted to make for a game or an app that could help others in some way. It was so exciting to see all these people, mostly girls younger than me, who were passionate about making something and making something that mattered. Their excitement to build made me excited to build, too. As nervous as I was feeling about my future and the "what next?" question, after each of these talks I felt inspired to do *something*. Especially something that made others feel and that moved them to positive action.

It's not that it was a new discovery. I've known that I wanted to use code to create positive social change; I've been saying that for years and for the last hundred pages of this book. But the book tour was like a slap-in-the-face reminder. Passion, really feeling energized about something, feels good. And instead of feeling nervous to get on stage or relief afterward that it was over, I just felt passionate. I was excited to share my story and excited to see that it could move and invigorate others.

This past year at college I've come to feel that incredible excited feeling with some of my projects. In one class, which was about mixing coding with language (I know that's vague but that was kind of the point: to let our c r e a t i v i t y shiiiiiiine), I got to express myself through coding. I explored telling a story through a series of images and prompts that guided the user to click on certain items. I made a game where you had to keep typing to push away a slime wall from falling down on your words and I used Markov chains to make a new journal out of a mash-up of my old ones. I got to make art through code and just like with *Tampon Run*, just like with writing this book, I got to make whatever funny idea I had into a reality.

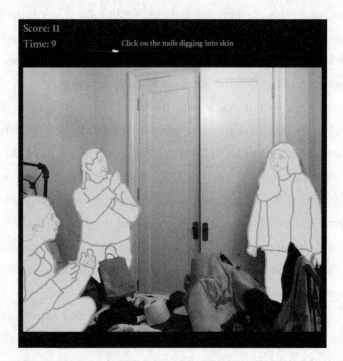

I wasn't just bringing my ideas to life through code or writing, I was getting to explore other mediums as well.

There are so many other ways to build and create. I learned to use the 3-D printer and the laser cutter at school. For my final project for one class, I made a 3-D printed square bra to make a point about the way bras, as we know them, create an arbitrary ideal breast shape, and then I wore it around. I laser cut my roommate's face into a fridge decal and then hung it on the fridge.

All these projects made me feel jittery and ALIVE and powerful and like I wanted to go, go, go, and make, make, make. You can't fake the drive that comes from being intensely passionate about something. And you can't fake the feeling of real passion. You know it when you feel it. So while this question of "what next?" still scares and haunts me and I still have no answer besides the vague one I've been saying for years ("coding + art + social change"), I realize I am on the correct path for me to figure that out. I'm a dog sniffing for the perfect spot to pee. I'm sniffing out the passion and when I find it, yes, I will stop there and metaphorically pee. And when I find something that makes me feel passionate in a big way, in a "let me devote myself and all my time to this idea or issue or movement" then that's what I'll do next.

Until then, aside from sniffing for a passion/pee spot, I'll be continuing to hone my coding skills while pushing myself to try new and uncomfortable situations. The summer before my freshman year, I trained at the Facebook University for Engineering program. It's a diversity program, meaning it's targeted at women and minorities in software engineering.

I spent eight weeks at Facebook's headquarters in California learning how to make Android apps and then built one myself.

This summer (before my sophomore year), I'll be returning to Facebook in New York as a software engineering intern. I'm scared! Like, actually scared! I still sometimes worry that I don't know how to code. Or worry that I'm bad at it. Or in my darkest hours worry that I only got this internship because I did their diversity program last summer, which I only got into because I made this little game when I was seventeen and people found it and liked it, so now I'm here with a Facebook internship (one of the best and hardest to get for a computer science college student) and worry that I have no idea how to code anything.

My thought process whenever I've gotten up on stage to talk about empowerment is you can't be afraid to fail and you have to believe in yourself. But I sometimes do a mental shrug and a mental giggle and a mental "Whatever, cause I'm here and in a few weeks I'm showing up at the Facebook office anyway and I'm gonna just do the best I can do." I am living the "just try" attitude. Because there's no way those feelings of "I'm an imposter" or "I have no idea what's going on" will ever disappear. All I can do, and all anyone else who feels this way can do, is just to plow on defiantly. Like this emoticon: ¯_(ツ)_/¯. One of my friends the other day told me that whenever she feels uncomfortable in a social situation or unsure of herself she just decides not to. I loved that.

And in the same vein, when I feel self-doubt I just decide to ¯_(ツ)_/¯ instead.

I'll be ¯_(ツ)_/¯-ing all the way through the summer and then, in the fall, I'll be ¯_(ツ)_/¯-ing in Berlin. I realized that to answer the "what next?" question I needed to sniff outside of my normal sniffing grounds. Outside of Brown University, outside of anything I already knew or had experienced. I don't know what I'll be doing in Berlin yet and I only know two people there, but I'm making it my home from September to January! And that's the point.

I try to imagine what sixteen-year-old Sophie would think about this plan (or really this non-plan). I don't think she would be very happy. Sixteen-year-old Sophie was afraid to fail to the point where she couldn't give a seven-minute English presentation without crying. Sixteen-year-old Sophie needed to get straight As. Sixteen-year-old Sophie would not move to a new place alone with no plan. But this is me now. This is Sophie, now in June 2017, almost twenty years old. And this Sophie, after making a game that went viral, after writing a book, after going on a book tour, after two years of computer science in college, this Sophie has learned to not fear failing, to push herself out of her comfort zone, to just do it even if she's scared, to ¯_(ツ)_/¯. So *entspann dich* ("peace out" in German according to Google Translate, yay for tech!)!!!!

ANDY

All within a few days and smack in the middle of my senior year of high school, I finished a ten-page economics paper, brusquely hurled applications at colleges, and dove headfirst into writing my first *Girl Code* chapter. As soon as we started writing, Sophie and I hit the ground running. We wrote the book at breakneck speed, sprinting to meet a deadline only a few months away. Even when I thought we'd finished the manuscript, we jumped straight into editing, ping-ponging iteration after iteration of the book between the two of us and our editor. I had submitted all my college applications, but still juggled my extracurricular activities and classes along with writing. By the time senior year came to a close, I felt swept up into it all: high school graduation, finishing the book, preparing to go to college, *and* getting over my big breakup (whoops).

Suddenly, it all fell away. Most of the book editing ended around the same time high school did, I knew where I was going to school in the fall, and I didn't have to see Nate anymore. My entire summer lay before me . . . and I had nothing to do. That summer, I made the active choice not to do another internship before I started school. As much as I had loved the past couple of years, they had taken a toll on me, and I desperately needed that full stop to really access my support network of friends and family and prepare for the next big phase of my life. I still thrived off constantly doing projects, and that summer I had a project—but that project was to focus on me.

By the time fall came around, I was refreshed, rejuvenated, and ready to start my freshman year at two universities: the University of North Carolina at Chapel Hill and Duke University. I was accepted to the Robertson Scholars Leadership Program, a joint program between UNC and Duke University. I have full student privileges at both campuses, and I can pursue majors and minors at both universities. Not only that, but the Robertson scholarship is paying for my college tuition, room and board, and other related fees.

*The first time I met the Robertson Scholars Leadership Program,
Class of 2020 (my class)!*

I am so grateful to *Tampon Run* for this. After working on the game and speaking about it for so long, I was
a full-fledged advocate—for women, young people, and
minorities, especially in the tech sector. When my interviews
for the scholarship came around, talking about my passion
for advocacy and social activism came easily because I had
already been doing it for so long. Writing the book gave me
the opportunity to reflect on myself and what I wanted to
do with my future, and helped me articulate to the admis-
sions panel what I was passionate about. The cost of college
in America is far from pocket change, and its hefty price tag

always lingered in the back of my and my family's minds. The work I did for *Tampon Run* has *completely eliminated* that problem for me, which, three years ago, I never would have expected. Seeing that *Tampon Run* has given back to my family in such a significant way adds to just how rewarding this whole journey has been, trials and tribulations and all.

Currently, I'm a declared computer science and journalism major at UNC, and I hope to declare a certificate (minor) in ~Arts of the Moving Image~ (film studies) at Duke University.

After everything, a computer science major came naturally. The journalism major and the film minor? Not so much. Within the journalism major, I'm following a multimedia track, which focuses on using technology and different forms of digital media to tell a story. And my AMI minor at Duke will give me the opportunity to learn more about how other people tell stories and how I could use film techniques to tell my own stories. I never expected to end up in a situation where I would be stacking a bunch of degrees on top of one another, and I'm still not sure how they'll come together into a career. But taking a step back and looking at the degrees that I've taken on: I'm not just interested in computer science, I'm interested in storytelling. Through my advocacy for women and minorities and in meeting people throughout my *Tampon Run* journey, I've realized that everybody has a story to tell but not everybody has the means to.

Up until this point, I've used coding and writing to tell stories. Through the book, I've encouraged people to find their
voices and tell their stories through code. As I learn more
about computer science and technology, I can build up my
arsenal to both tell stories and teach people how to tell stories
in even more interesting and varied ways.

Computer science in college is different and a lot more
difficult—not just because of the information that we're
learning. I started in the level above the intro class (COMP
401). On the first day, the class was full of excited freshman,
sophomores, and juniors! But as the weeks went on and people dropped out of the course, I found myself in a lecture hall
of about eighty students and . . . maybe ten of them were
women. Most of us sat in a half-hearted cluster on the left.
Our professor would give a lecture for half of the class, and for
the other half, we were supposed to work with our classmates
and TAs (teaching assistants). I completely slinked back into
my old habits, brooding over my problem sets alone, unwill-
ing to discuss them with anyone else. But I was clearly not
making the same progress I would have if I had asked TAs or
my peers for help. I was intimidated somehow! Intimidated
by all the men in the room, by all the people who seemed
to live and breathe code on another level. As the end of the
course neared, I realized that I wasn't meeting the academic
expectations that I had set up for myself. It wasn't because
I wasn't capable of learning the material, it was just that I

didn't seek out the same help that I needed. I had to face the fear I had of asking questions, working with someone else, and failing in order to approach my TA for assistance. After that, I spent hours and hours with my TA, sitting late into the night with him—only then did I get the learning experience and time that I needed to really understand the material.

And as I've been selecting courses for the major, it's becoming even clearer to me that computer science is not just programming. Think about a square. A square is a type of rectangle, but a rectangle is not equivalent to a square. In the same way programming is a part of computer science, but computer science is not just programming. There are a lot of studies within computer science that don't involve programming at all, and instead examine what computers can do. Computer science is a lot more theoretical and programming is less abstract—it's like the difference between architecture and construction. But currently, I haven't even gotten that far in my CS education to truly experience that distinction!

Fast-forward to March 2017. I'm hurriedly walking back to my college dorm room, carrying a deceptively heavy package. Despite the weight, I'm moving quickly. Emblazoned on the package's label is a return address from HarperCollins Publishers, and for the first time ever, I'm starting to realize that Sophie and I have written a book. I hustle into my dorm room, rip through the packaging, and I open the box to find two neatly arranged stacks of hardcover copies of our book.

So I cried.

I cried from the joy of being a published author. I cried from relief, for in that box was the final book—no more edits, no more changes. And I cried from sadness. The past few years, I had learned so much about myself and the world around me, and it wasn't until I saw a two hundred-something-page book about it that I fully understood just how much we had learned and done. It was weird to think that, after writing the book, Sophie and I were potentially nearing the end of a three-year adventure together.

The day after the book hit the shelves, I flew out to meet Sophie, beginning an almost picturesque way of bookending our *Tampon Run/Girl Code*–related time together: the *Girl Code* book tour.

At one of our stops, Sophie and I were sitting at this long table of authors and people lined up to get their books signed. We wrapped up signing around the same time these two authors next to us were about to leave their tables: Dean Hale and Shannon Hale. Shannon Hale . . . I couldn't believe it. Shannon Hale had written *The Goose Girl*—one of my absolute favorite books when I was in middle school. It's this fantasy, coming-of-age story about a princess who finds that she has these powers, reclaims her kingdom, and saves her prince. *The Goose Girl* was one of many books featuring young women coming into their own and becoming empowered; it immensely influenced me as a reader, and seeing the force behind it all overwhelmed me.

I was beside myself with excitement. I sprang out of my chair and scrambled to get around the table to reach her.

"Hi Mrs. Hale I'm really sorry to interrupt I know you were just leaving I'm an author here." I gestured wildly to where Sophie and I sat. "I just wanted to say that I really loved *The Goose Girl* it was one of my favorite books when I was younger and I was wondering if I could have your autograph maybe if that's okay?"

As Mrs. Hale warmly assented, I scanned the nearby area for something she could sign. In desperation, I grasped at my own author name placard from the signing table and held it out to her with the Sharpie I used to sign *my* books. On the placard, Mrs. Hale scribbled her autograph and passed it back to me. I thanked her profusely as she left with her husband and, in a daze, I wandered back to my seat at the authors' table.

Above Mrs. Hale's (beautifully written) signature read, "You're a reader worth writing for!"

I laughed. In that moment, I understood what it felt like to be in awe of someone. I didn't realize it when I first read *The Goose Girl*, but Mrs. Hale's writing clearly influenced what I believe about women and strength now. Readers can extract so much from the books they consume—*I* was one of those readers as a child and I still am. But until I was on tour, I wasn't used to thinking that my book could hold the same weight for others. And as Sophie and I traveled, we saw and met young readers who were impacted by *Girl Code* and our story.

As we toured, we interacted with hundreds of young readers. At first they seemed shy and nervous when asking questions, afraid when they approached us for autographs. But as an event or conversation went on, they all blossomed into remarkably engaging, inquisitive, and ambitious people . . .

people who admired us. That still feels unreal and almost undeserved. I'm still a normal person! I was in the middle of my first year in college! It was weird having to break down this invisible wall between us and our readers, and it was weird to think that girls felt toward me and Sophie the same feelings I had felt toward someone I admired, like Mrs. Hale. It also contradicted my own insecurities—I was scared to believe that I could be admired. Admitting that admiration was even possible made me feel like I had an inflated ego, and I wasn't ready to believe I was someone worth admiring. It felt so disorienting to think that I was someone people could look up to because when I looked out at our excited, breathless readers, I felt that every one of them had the capacity to be the author of a book *I* would one day read.

I loved meeting our readers, and I really learned so much from meeting them in their hometowns. At each of our tour stops, we visited a number of schools. Back in New York, Sophie and I had gone to schools with similar environments, so going around the country and seeing different snippets of other school environments was incredibly eye-opening. Each of the schools we visited had different access to resources and had vastly different student body demographics. Some of the schools we visited didn't have the nice facilities or the means that other schools did. My schools had contributed so much to supporting me as I grew and found my voice. Going on tour and physically being in and experiencing different learning environments helped me understand that not every school can offer that same support because some schools are just trying to stay open.

For me, a big aspect of growing up as a first-generation immigrant was money. It's true that my whole family always worries about finances, but I never had to consider working a job while I was at school, or sacrificing my education to make ends meet at home. And yes, my parents wanted me to be a "doctor, lawyer, or engineer," but with that pressure they also assured me that they'd make it work so they could pay for that education. It definitely wasn't easy at times, but in some ways, I was incredibly lucky to have grown up in the communities and with the opportunities that I did.

Regardless of what school or bookstore or city Sophie and I visited, I was awestruck by the drive and earnestness with which all our readers approached their futures, both in tech and in life. Whatever obstacles they had in school or at home, they continued to search for their voices, and the causes they wanted to fight for. Not all of them had found their voices yet, but they knew they had them inside. So many of them were learning to code so they could speak out, make an impact, and make a difference. On the tour, I realized that even though I had been working as an advocate for women and minorities in tech for three years, the foundation for my voice was built much earlier on. Code is so readily available to anyone with access to a computer, even more than when I was growing up. The gusto with which these young people approached code as a tool for changing the world blew me away, and I saw that the impact that Sophie and I made is only a sampling of what future programmers and activists have to offer.

The first stop on our book tour was at the Bertha Means Sadler Middle School in Austin, Texas. It was amazing to meet our readers!

CODING APPENDIX

Now that you've finished the book, we imagine you're feeling pretty excited to get coding. Well, the great news is nearly everyone has access to code! You have access to it right now if you're near a computer. In the pages that follow, we're going to give you the steps to code your own "Hello World" program (just like we talked about in our story) and show you a few other nifty tricks in Python. As we mentioned before, Python is the coding language that most resembles English and is good for building Web applications, testing programs, making video games . . . generally anything. A lot of major technology companies use it.

We know this might sound crazy, but everything that runs

on code, no matter how complex, is just a combination of the fundamentals you'll be learning about and working with in this appendix: conditional statements (if/else statements), functions, loops, and variables. Normally, coders start with the problem they want to solve with code and then they figure out how to put together the fundamentals to solve that problem. Their next step is typing the code into a text editor on their computer, like Sublime or Eclipse (which is basically Word for writing and editing code). The computer itself reads and carries out the code. Programs (a fancy word for a set of coded instructions that do a specific task) can sometimes make physical things happen, like making a robot move or making your keyboard light up when it gets dark. These outcomes are the result of complex interactions between software, which is all the code, and hardware, which are all the physical things like the actual wires and voltage in the robot or your computer. We're not going to be making robots or keyboard light shows in this appendix, but we *are* going to take you through steps so that you can make choose-your-own-adventure and decision-making programs. If you want to get the most out of this appendix, don't just follow the instructions blindly: try to understand *why* you're doing each step and think about all the other ways you could put these fundamentals together to code anything, big or small. We've also included a table at the beginning to define some key terms, many of which you're already familiar with after reading the book.

Before doing any of these activities, you'll need to set up Python on your computer. Python is not a new language, though every once in a while the Python Software Foundation releases new versions of the language. In these coding tutorials, we will be using Python 2.7. Python 2.7 will be compatible with all future versions of Python, but Python 3 will NOT. DO NOT DOWNLOAD PYTHON 3.

We recommend searching "download Python 2.7 for Mac" or "download Python 2.7 for PC" in Google and clicking one of the top links. When you download Python, by default you also will also download IDLE (Integrated DeveLopment Environment or Integrated Development and Learning Environment), which is a computer application that will produce a white screen where you will input your own code. Per the first sentence of this paragraph, you'll need to download a different version of Python depending on the type of platform you're using (Mac, Windows, etc.), but it should only take a few clicks to get your computer ready. Once you finish the download process, you can find IDLE by searching your computer for the word "IDLE" or by looking around in your applications or downloads folder. You don't actually have to "open" Python; once you've downloaded it, the language is there. You only need to open IDLE. So get Python on your computer, open IDLE, and let's get started!

IMPORTANT TERMS!	DEFINITIONS
Programming Language	In real life, people can communicate with each other using different languages, like Spanish, Mandarin, or Hindi. Programmers communicate with computers by writing code in a **programming language**, like Java or Python. When we made *Tampon Run*, we used a language called JavaScript.
Bugs	**Bugs** are problems in your code. They're either syntax errors (you mistyped something and the computer doesn't understand you) or logic errors (the computer follows your instructions but they don't solve the problem you wanted). Sometimes bugs make your program act in weird ways and sometimes bugs make it not run at all. Instead you'll just get an error message. Going through your code to fix these issues is called **debugging** (the term came from when programmers had to remove actual bugs from their computer.)

Libraries	**Libraries** are like a spice rack. Instead of buying all the spices whole and taking the time to grind each one out every time you make a new dish, you can just buy a spice rack full of jars of ground spices, and the job's done for you. You can use all sorts of spices at your convenience. **Libraries** are collections of prewritten code. Programmers can use the code from **libraries** to make writing programs simpler for them, since coding even simple things can be hard to do. For example, lots of coders might want to use buttons in their programs so a user can interact with the product. But it doesn't make sense for everyone to rewrite the code to make a button every time. Instead a coder can import premade button code.

ProcessingJS	We used the library **ProcessingJS** to make *Tampon Run* because it made coding graphics (i.e., getting pictures to actually show up on the screen) easier for us. Instead of typing multiple lines of code to create a rectangle on-screen, we would just type drawRect().
Documentation	Using libraries isn't always that easy, and that's where **documentation** comes in. It's like an online instruction manual or guide to using all the code that comes in a library.

BASIC CODING STRUCTURES/ COMMANDS	DEFINITIONS
Variables	**Variables** are how you store information in your code. They make it easy to refer to data later. For example you could store your height in a variable called "height." If you grew the next year you could update the number stored in "height." And whenever you wanted to refer to your height you could just refer to the variable "height." More on variables in the guide following this table.
Lists	In your daily life you might make a grocery list of foods or a to-do list of tasks. Similarly, you can make virtual **lists** with code and they can be filled with any piece of information. Whereas variables store single pieces of information, lists hold multiple related pieces of information. Just like you might number the items in your grocery list 1, 2, 3, each item in a virtual list has a number depending where it is in the list.

EXAMPLE CODE

Variable storing number:

```
height = 68
```

Variable storing string:

```
greatestPerson = "Sophie"
```

```
food0 = "nutella"
food1 = "fluff"
food2 = "mushrooms"

groceryList = [food0, food1, food2]
```

Conditionals	**Conditionals** allow computers to decide which instructions to follow depending on whether a true/false statement is true or false. If I were to use one in conversation, I could say, "If you're happy, clap your hands. Else, frown."
Loops	There are times when a programmer wants a computer to do something a bunch of times; for example, draw 300 rectangles. But it's confusing and inefficient to write 300 lines of code that say "draw a rectangle." Instead, we'll use a **loop** to tell the computer, "draw a rectangle 300 times." In this case we'll use a "for loop." By putting "drawRect()" indented in the example on the right, we're telling the computer to do that piece of code 300 times.

```
if (x == 1):
    print("x is 1! YAAY!")
else:
    print("x is not 1! :( sry bb.")
```

• == in code means "is the thing on the left equal to the thing on the right?"

• = in code means store the thing on the right in the thing on the left

```
for i in range (0, 300):
    drawRect()
```

| Functions | Instead of asking someone to take out a pan and take out the eggs and turn the flame on and so on and so on, we just say "make me an egg." If a person doesn't know how, they can look up the steps online. In the same way, **functions** define how to do something for a computer. Once you've defined how to do it once, you can just refer to the function by name in other parts of the program and the computer will look up your definition from earlier to understand what to do. This process of simply referring to the function by name after you've defined it elsewhere is called "calling a function." |

We're defining the function friendlyHello. Depending on the result of the random number generator, it will print out a different friendly hello.

```python
def friendlyHello():
    import random
    number = random.randint(1, 2)
    if (number == 1):
        print("Wazzzup")
    else:
        print("Ahoy!")
```

WRITE A HELLO WORLD PROGRAM

Let's write our first program! While working on this section, you'll learn how to:
- Write a simple program using Python
- Save your simple program and run it

Let's get started!

1. Open IDLE. A Python Shell window will open. From now on, the Python Shell window will display whatever you make your program print (in other words, "show") to the screen or any bugs the computer encounters when running your program.
2. Leave that for now and, at the top of your computer screen, click **File ➜ New File**. This File window will be where you type all your code.
3. Let's start by writing some code in a file, and then we'll actually run the code. In the File window (NOT the Python Shell window) type:

```
print("Hello world!")
```

In this line, you're telling the computer that you want it to print out exactly what's in the quotes. Note that nothing will print yet because you haven't told the computer to actually follow the instructions you've typed.

4. Next, let's save that code in your file so the computer can read it later. At the top of your screen, click **File → Save**. In the Save As box, type the name of the file (`myprogram.py` would be a good name). Whatever you name it, make sure the file name ends in .py—this lets the computer know this is a Python file, which is important because the computer will behave differently knowing it's reading Python and not some other coding language.

5. Finally, let's run the code in your file. At the top of your screen, click **Run → Run Module**. This tells the computer to follow the instructions in your file. If it worked you should see the following in the Python Shell window (NOT the File window):

`Hello world!`

6. Pat yourself on the back! You've just written your first program! (If it didn't work, make sure that you typed everything *exactly as we wrote it above*.)

DEBUGGING A STORY PROGRAM

Now let's write a program that tells a story (and that also has a few bugs in it—on purpose. We want you to see what happens when a program has bugs)! While working on this section, you'll learn how to:

- Write a program that contains multiple lines of code
- Debug a program with syntax errors
- Recognize common syntax errors

1. In your File window (NOT your Python Shell window) type the following program EXACTLY:

line	
01:	`print("Once upon a time")`
02:	`PRint("there were two dope ladies")`
03:	`print("named Sophie and Andy.")`
04:	`print(They wanted to learn to code")`
05:	`print("and nothing would stop them!"`

2. Let's run the code in your new file. At the top of your screen, click **Run ➜ Run Module**. What happens? Check your computer screen. Don't skip ahead! We'll still be here when you get back :-).

    If you copied this code EXACTLY, you will get an error from Python—more specifically, it should say **Invalid**

Syntax. This is just a fancy way of saying that you typed something that the computer can't understand.

3. Let's fix the bug. Which line of code do you think caused the problem? Why? Don't skip ahead—really make a guess. Learning to code is about learning to think, and right now you need to spend some time thinking. As always, we'll be here when you've made your guess.

The first problematic line that we noticed was Line 02. We typed `PRint`, but we seem to have spelled it using two uppercase letters at the beginning. Unfortunately, computers aren't very smart and can only follow very exact instructions. The computer knows what `print` means in Python, but it doesn't know what `PRint` means. Let's be more specific and fix Line 02 by replacing it with the following code:

```
print("there were two dope ladies")
```

4. Once you've fixed the bug, let's test our fix to see if it works. At the top of your screen, click **Run → Run Module**. What happens?

Nooooooo! Another syntax error! Which line of code do you think is causing the problem now? Why? Make a guess!

The problematic line of code that we noticed was Line 04. It seems like we forgot the opening quotes. A good rule to remember is that quotes should always come in pairs—an opening one and a closing one. Let's fix Line 04 by replacing it with the following code:

```
print("They wanted to learn to code")
```

5. Once you've fixed that bug, let's test our new fix to see if it works. At the top of your screen, click **Run** ➔ **Run Module**. What happens?

Aoeifhaogehaowegh! Another syntax error! Which line of code do you think caused the problem? Why? Make a guess!

The problematic line of code that we noticed was Line 05. Line 05 has a very similar problem to Line 04. It seems like we forgot a closing parenthesis. This is really common. As we said, a good rule to remember is that parentheses should always come in pairs—an opening one and a closing one. Let's fix Line 05 by replacing it with the following code:

```
print("and nothing would stop them!")
```

6. Can you predict what comes next? Well, now that you've fixed the bugs, let's test our new fix to see if it works. You'll notice that we did this in Step 4 and Step 5, and now we're doing it again in Step 6. This pattern of repeatedly fixing a bug and testing the fix and finding a new bug and fixing the new bug and testing the new fix and finding ANOTHER new bug and fixing this OTHER new bug and so on is called debugging, and it's really common when writing code. Bugs are normal and should be expected. Never get discouraged! This happens to the best coders.

So, back to checking to see if our new fix works. At the top of your screen, click **Run ➜ Run Module**. What happens?

If you've fixed everything, you should see the following in the Python Shell window (NOT the File window):

```
Once upon a time
there were two dope ladies
named Sophie and Andy.
They wanted to learn to code
and nothing would stop them!
```

7. Do a victory dance! You just fixed three bugs! Now, take some time to create a completely new story by putting your own made-up lines between the quotes of the print command. Feel free to add more than five print lines if you want. See if you encounter any other types of bugs while you work.

ASKING FOR INPUT

Let's write a program that tells a story and allows someone else to change parts of the story (without them actually writing any of the code)! Delete everything you wrote in the last activity from your file and start on line 1. Alternatively, if you want to save your work from the last activity, create an entirely new file. While working on this section, you'll learn how to:

- Declare and initialize a variable
- Use a function to get user input
- Concatenate a string variable and a string literal

1. To start, we're going to write a program that looks very similar to our previous story program. However, we're going to add a few things that you haven't seen before. If you're not sure what they mean, that's okay. We're going to explain them. In your File window (NOT

your Python Shell window) type the following program
EXACTLY, hitting Enter at the end of each line to start
the next line:

line	
01:	`print("I want to tell you a story about two girls,")`
02:	`print("but I need your help to tell the story!")`
03:	`adj = raw_input("Pick a fun word to describe the girls! ")`
04:	`girl_a = raw_input("What is the name of the first girl? ")`
05:	`girl_b = raw_input("What's the second girl's name? ")`
06:	`thing = raw_input("What are they going to learn about? ")`
07:	`print("The Story of " + girl_a + " and " + girl_b + "*")`
08:	`print("Once upon a time")`
09:	`print("there were two " + adj + " ladies")`
10:	`print("named " + girl_a + " and " + girl_b + ".")`
11:	`print("They wanted to learn " + thing)`
12:	`print("and nothing would stop them!")`

2. Let's run the code in your file. At the top of your screen, click **Run ➔ Run Module**. What happens? Check your computer screen. Don't skip ahead! We'll still be here when you get back :-).

    In the Python Shell window (NOT the File window), you should see:

    ```
    I want to tell you a story about two girls,
    but I need your help to tell the story!
    Pick a fun word to describe the girls!
    ```

    You'll notice that your cursor (the little blinking vertical line) is hanging out at the end of the last sentence. The program is waiting for the user to enter a word! In the Python Shell window, type in a fun word to describe the girls and then hitting Enter. For example:

    ```
    I want to tell you a story about two girls,
    but I need your help to tell the story!
    Pick a fun word to describe the girls! AWESOME
    ```

3. Then hit Enter. You should see the following in your Python Shell window:

    ```
    I want to tell you a story about two girls,
    but I need your help to tell the story!
    ```

```
Pick a fun word to describe the girls! AWESOME
What is the name of the first girl?
```

The program is waiting for the user to enter a word again. In the Python Shell window, type in a name for the first girl and then hit Enter. For example:

```
I want to tell you a story about two girls,
but I need your help to tell the story!
Pick a fun word to describe the girls! AWESOME
What is the name of the first girl? Grace
```

4. Using the same process, pick a name for the second girl and the thing they are going to learn about. We chose Ada and math. So our Python Shell window looked like this just before we hit Enter after typing math:

```
I want to tell you a story about two girls,
but I need your help to tell the story!
Pick a fun word to describe the girls! AWESOME
What is the name of the first girl? Grace
What's the second girl's name? Ada
What are they going to learn about? math
```

5. Now let's hit Enter. What printed out on your screen after you hit Enter? Don't skip ahead! Check your computer screen. We'll still be here when you get back :-).

Our program printed out the following:

```
*The Story of Grace and Ada*
Once upon a time
there were two AWESOME ladies
named Grace and Ada.
They wanted to learn math
and nothing would stop them!
```

6. Run the program again (go to your File window and clicking **Run ➜ Run Module**). This time, pick a different fun word, different names, and a different thing to learn about. Really! Try something different! We'll be here when you get back :-).

7. So what's going on here? The first thing we'll need to look at is raw_input. The first time we encounter this is on Line 03:

```
adj = raw_input("Pick a fun word to describe the
girls!")
```

raw_input is a function, which is stored code that someone has already written that you can customize and use again and again. In this case, when we called this function and customized it with the message "Pick a fun word to describe the girls!" `raw_input` will show the custom message on the screen. Then `raw_input` does something interesting: it waits for someone to type something into the Python Shell window *before* moving on with the rest of the program.

After someone types in a word and hits Enter, `raw_input` takes whatever the user typed into the Python Shell and hands it back to the program. So when we typed `AWESOME` the first time, raw_input took `AWESOME` from the Python Shell window and literally put the string `AWESOME` into our program. More specifically, it stored the string `AWESOME` into a variable named `adj`. Think of `adj` like a storage box. You can put any word inside of it that you want to save for later.

8. Now that we stored the word the user typed, let's use that word! In our story, we don't want to use the word that describes the girls until the third line of the story. So let's take a look at Line 09 in the code where this happens:

```
print("there were two " + adj + " ladies")
```

In this line of code, we are using whatever string was stored in the variable `adj`. That means that when the computer runs this line of code, it is NOT going to print

adj to the screen. Instead it's going to print whatever is stored in **adj**. In our example this was **AWESOME**. If we run the program again it could be any other word you want (**FANTASTIC** or **AMAZING** or **FUN** or **HEROIC**).

To make it clear to the computer that we want to print what's stored in **adj**, we make sure that we do not put it in quotes. However, because we want what's stored in **adj** to appear between the string literal **"there were two "** and the string literal **" ladies"**, we have to insert it between the two with the + sign. This is called concatenation, and is just a fancy name for sticking strings together.

9.   We used this same pattern to allow the user to pick the girls' names and the thing they want to learn:

   •   Call the **raw_input** function to prompt the user with a question or statement
   •   Store the string value returned by the **raw_input** function in a variable
   •   Concatenate the string value in the variable with string literals and print out the result

If you want, come up with your own story with different parts that a user can choose! Do this by changing what's in between the quotes of the print and **raw_input** functions. You can also add or take away `raw_input` lines, variables and the way lines are concatenated. Just use the pattern described above.

MAKING CHOICES

Let's write a program that allows the computer to make a decision about what a user should do given a set of user input. While working on this section, you'll learn how to:

- Use flowcharts to plan programs that can make choices
- Translate a flowchart into a series of conditional statements to allow the computer to make a choice

1. To start, we're going to think about a problem everyone has in the morning—"Should I sleep in or should I wake up?" The answer to that question depends on many things—whether or not you're feeling sick, whether or not it's the weekend, whether or not it's summer, etc. Let's simplify the problem and pretend that the decision only depends on three questions:
   - Is it a weekend or a weekday?
   - Is it summer or is school in session?
   - Is it a holiday or not?

In this chart, each diamond is a question that must be answered. The only way someone is allowed to answer each question is by choosing an answer next to one of the lines coming out from the diamond. Then the person should follow the arrow to either a final decision (the rounded box) or another question. These charts are called flowcharts and help us conceptualize what we'll actually be coding. Below is an example of a flowchart we could make to solve the problem of sleeping in or waking up:

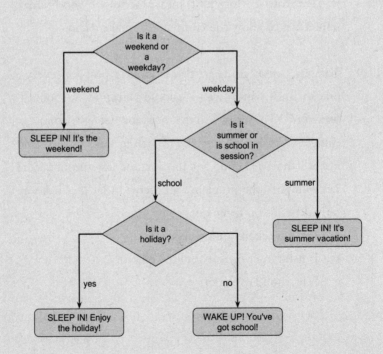

One really crucial thing to note is that you follow this chart in order. If you follow it correctly you must ask yourself "Is it a weekend or a weekday?" first. And if you answer "weekend" to that question, you will never ask yourself any other question because you arrive at one final answer. This is going to be really important for writing a program that solves the problem "Should I sleep in or should I wake up?"

2. Next, let's write the program that simulates this flow-chart. In this program, we'll need to indent certain lines of code. Indenting just means that you start a line of code further to the right. When writing in Python we'll hit the Tab key (NOT the spacebar) whenever we're trying to indent. If you accidentally type spaces where you need tabs, you might get a syntax error. Also, to help you know how many tabs we indent, we've added a helpful ruler at the top and bottom of the code that measures out how many tabs you need (we'll explain more on why you need indentation later on). Alright, let's get coding. Type the following into the Python Shell window:

LINE	0 tabs	1 tab	2 tabs	3 tabs
01:	print("It's 7:00 AM. You're in bed.")			
02:	print("Should you sleep in or wake up?")			
03:	print("**START**")			
04:	print("Is it a weekend or a weekday?")			
05:	day_type = raw_input("Type 'weekend' or 'weekday': ")			
06:	if day_type == "weekend":			
07:		print("SLEEP IN! It's the weekend.")		
08:	else:			
09:		print("Is it summer or is school in session?")		
10:		time_of_yr = raw_input("Type 'school' or 'summer': ")		
11:		if time_of_yr == "school":		
12:			print("Is it a holiday?")	
13:			holiday = raw_input("Type 'yes' or 'no': ")	
14:			if holiday == "yes":	

LINE	0 tabs	1 tab	2 tabs	3 tabs
15:				print("SLEEP IN! Enjoy the holiday!")
16:			else:	
17:				print("WAKE UP! You've got school!")
18:		else:		
19:			print("SLEEP IN! It's summer vacation!")	

3. So let's break this down. In Line 01 through Line 03 our program explains the situation to the user and lets them know the questions are about to begin.

Then on Line 04 the program prints out the very first question the flowchart asks.

On Line 05 the program calls the `raw_input` function to tell the user that only "weekend" and "weekday" are acceptable answers and also gets the user's answer. The program stores the answer to that question in a variable named `day_type`.

On Line 06 the program has its first conditional statement. A conditional statement is a line of code that lets the program choose to run or not run another line of code based on a boolean expression (which is an expression that evaluates to either be true or false). In this case the boolean expression on Line 06 is `day_type == "weekend"`. This piece of code tells the computer to compare the string stored in the `day_type` variable to the string `"weekend"`. When the two are the same, this boolean expression will evaluate to True. When they are not the same, this boolean expression will evaluate to False. The conditional statement (all of Line 06 including the `if` and the `:`) then uses the result of the boolean expression to decide what line of code to run next. If the boolean expression is True the program will go to Line 07. Can you guess where the program will go to if the boolean expression is False? Guess before you read ahead!

If the boolean expression is False, the program will next go to Line 08. After the computer reaches the **else:**, it will then continue on to the next line under the else (Line 09).

The indentation tells the computer which code should happen in each situation. Line 07 should only be performed if the boolean expression in Line 06 is True because it's indented under it. Likewise, Line 09 should only be performed if we get to Line 08 because it's indented under the **else:**.

The combination of Line 06 and Line 08 is called an if-else statement. It allows the computer to perform one set of actions or another set of actions but never both.

4. Let's test our understanding of the rest of the program. Pretend that the user runs the program and types **weekday** as a response to the first question and **vacation** as a response to the second, like this:

```
It's 7:00 AM. You're in bed.
Should you sleep in or wake up?
**START**
Is it a weekend or a weekday?
Type 'weekend' or 'weekday': weekday
Is it summer or is school in session?
Type 'school' or 'summer': vacation
```

What will the program print out next? Make a guess! Or run the program and check! Either way, do the work! This thinking part is really important.

Even though we input a different answer than the two options, "school" or "summer," the program will still print out the following:

```
SLEEP IN! It's summer vacation!
```

But why? Let's look at the code. If the user types **vacation** and hits Enter, this means the string **"vacation"** gets stored in the **time_of_yr** variable on Line 10.

The program next goes to the conditional on Line 11. That conditional contains the boolean expression **time_of_yr == "school"**. Because the **time_of_yr** variable is storing **"vacation"**, this boolean expression will evaluate to False. This means the conditional on Line 11 will cause the computer to next go to Line 18. After the computer reaches the **else:**, it will then continue on to the next line under the else (Line 19).

In the previous example we tried answering one of the questions (**Is it summer or is school in session?**) with an answer we weren't supposed to use (**vacation** instead of **summer** or **school**). What happens if we answer the first question (**Is it a weekend or a weekday?**) with **WEEKEND** (all capitals?). Run the program and input the following:

```
It's 7:00 AM. You're in bed.
Should you sleep in or wake up?
**START**
Is it a weekend or a weekday?
Type 'weekend' or 'weekday': WEEKEND
```

What happens after you hit Enter? Try it out!

In this case, the program then prints out the following:

```
Is it summer or is school in session?
Type 'school' or 'summer':
```

Why did the program ask you about school and summer? Didn't you just tell the program that it was the weekend? Shouldn't it tell you `SLEEP IN! It's the weekend.`? Well, in this case, it turns out the boolean expression on Line 06 (`day_type == "weekend"`) will evaluate to False because capital `"WEEKEND"` (what the user typed in) is not the same as lowercase `"weekend"` (what is in the code). Computers are very precise about following instructions. If you program it to tell you if something is the same (by using ==), then the computer is going to tell you whether or not things are EXACTLY the same.

6. Take some time to re-run your program several times with different answers to each question each time. See if you can get the program to print out every possible final answer (e.g. `SLEEP IN! It's the weekend.`, `SLEEP IN! Enjoy the holiday!`, `WAKE UP! You've got school!`, and `SLEEP IN! It's summer vacation!`).

7. If you want, come up with your own flowchart with different choices and different answers and translate it into a program.

Or, if you want more practice with our help, try to translate our flowchart below into a program. This flowchart is designed to help people choose a pet. You should try to translate the flowchart to a program on your own first, and then, if you need help, you can look ahead for the program that we wrote. Here's the flowchart:

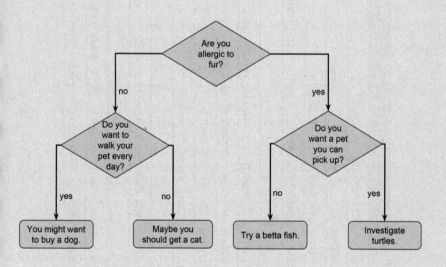

LINE	0 tabs	1 tab	2 tabs
01:	`print("Get help choosing a pet!")`		
02:	`print("**START**")`		
03:	`print("Are you allergic to fur?")`		
04:	`allergic = raw_input("Answer 'yes' or 'no': ")`		
05:	`if allergic == "no":`		
06:		`print("Do you want to walk your pet every day?")`	
07:		`go_for_walk = raw_input("Answer 'yes' or 'no': ")`	
08:		`if go_for_walk == "yes":`	
09:			`print("You might want to buy a dog.")`
10:		`else:`	
11:			`print("Maybe you should get a cat.")`
12:	`else:`		
13:		`print("Do you want a pet you can pick up?")`	
14:		`hold = raw_input("Answer 'yes' or 'no': ")`	

LINE	0 tabs	1 tab	2 tabs
15:	if hold == "no":		
16:		print("Try a betta fish.")	
17:	else:		
18:		print("Investigate turtles.")	

These tutorials barely scratch the surface of what computer science has to offer. We want to tell you more, but there just aren't enough pages in the world, much less in this book, to cover how technology is improving, expanding, and changing every day. If you want to learn more, look online! There is a whole slew of resources waiting to be found by new programmers hungry to learn more. That's you.

Good luck, and congrats—you're a coder!

SOME RESOURCES IF YOU WANT TO LEARN MORE CODING SKILLS

GENERAL CODING INFORMATION

Girls Who Code: girlswhocode.com

Black Girls Who Code: blackgirlswhocode.com

CODING TUTORIALS

Codecademy: codecademy.com

Code.org: code.org

Lynda: Lynda.com

Khan Academy: khanacademy.org

ACKNOWLEDGMENTS

We couldn't have made it this far without the army of people who helped us. Over the past two years, so many people have provided overwhelming support and generosity.

First and foremost, we are so grateful to Reshma Saujani and Girls Who Code, the amazing organization she founded and is building. Reshma's dedication to empowering girls and bringing greater diversity to the tech world is extraordinary. *Tampon Run* exists thanks to Girls Who Code, where the two of us met, joyfully coded, and were encouraged to express ourselves freely. That warm, open, and supportive environment in our GWC class at IAC '14 existed thanks to our GWC instructor, Sean Stern, and the young women in our GWC class. They are the true day-one supporters of *Tampon Run*—without their support, we wouldn't have found the courage to make the game in the first place! And thank you, Sean, for guiding us on the appendix in this book so we could pass on the joy of coding to our readers.

We also want to thank Cheryl Houser, Sophie's mom. From the day *Tampon Run* went viral, she has guided and supported us, not just as Sophie's mom, but as our manager. She's helped us find our voice as professional adults and spoken for us when we weren't ready to advocate for ourselves. Cheryl has selflessly given hours and hours of her time to us, all while running her own production company! She's been not only a strong advocate for us, but an example for how we should act as businesswomen moving forward.

The iOS app never would have existed without the help of Nihal Mehta, Natalie Bartlett, and Pivotal Labs. Nihal, Reshma's husband, was a huge proponent of the iOS app, and connected us with development firm Pivotal Labs. Pivotal Labs devoted a full team of developers and designers to work on the app full time for seven weeks for free! There is absolutely, positively no way we could have created an app of that quality in seven weeks, much less ever, without that team. So thanks to Pivotal Labs, and to our team of Alex Basson, Sam Coward, Linda Joy, and Catherine McGarvey. And thanks to Drew Joy, our talented music composer for the app.

If writing a whole chapter on you guys didn't prove our

gratitude for you all, here's an official thank-you to Weeby.co for giving us one of our early transformative experiences and validating that women have a place at the coding table. And hearty thanks to the many other organizations and people that validated and helped us grow along the way, including Simple Machine, Craig Hatkoff, Irwin Kula and the team at the Tribeca Disruptive Innovators Awards, the Webbys, the Business Innovation Factory, DoSomething.org, Games for Change, many remarkable start-up founders and coders and venture capitalists, and many others.

And a huge shout-out, too, to our *Tampon Run* fans the world over. Thank you for emailing us, tweeting about us, writing about us, telling your friends about us, playing the game, and opening up and sharing your personal and emotional menstruation stories with us. The most rewarding aspect of our *Tampon Run* journey has been seeing how our wacky little game really did impact people everywhere and achieve what we set out to do: cause open discussion about menstruation to break down the taboo around it.

A big thanks to our publisher, HarperCollins, for making this book a reality, starting first and foremost with our wonderful editor, Sara Sargent (we'll never forget the cupcakes). As for the rest of the team, we are so grateful to you for your time and efforts, especially Anna Prendella, Stephanie Hoover, Sarah Kaufman, Emily Rader, Megan Gendell, Bess Braswell, Sabrina Abballe, Victor Hendrickson, Andrea

Pappenheimer, Kerry Moynagh, Kathy Faber, Jen Wygand, Heather Doss, Fran Olson, Jennifer Sheridan, Susan Yeager, and Deb Murphy. Thank you all for getting this book out there!

Thank you so much also to our wonderful agents, Mackenzie Brady Watson and Joanna Volpe, for reaching out to us when the game went viral and for encouraging, supporting, and wrangling us every step of the way. And to the rest of the incredible team at New Leaf Literary: Hilary Pecheone, Lauren Wohl, Mike Kelly, Jackie Lindert, Danielle Barthel, Kathleen Ortiz, Mia Roman, Pouya Shahbazian, and Chris McEwen.

ANDY:

Yo, I'mma let Sophie finish, but I had some of the best supporters of all time! Some of the best supporters of all time!

Ha-ha. I'm sorry.

I desperately need to thank my family. The past two years have been so hard for me, and so rewarding, and my parents and sisters have always been supportive of my decisions and my voice. You always made sure I was on top of my game, and when you thought I was spreading myself too thin, called me out for it. Shouts-out to my BEST. FRIENDS. Russell, Jeffers, and everyone in Ned's—I hit a lot of highs and lows as I pushed through schoolwork, college applications, and *Tampon Run* stuff. You all, and my other amazing friends, have been with me through thick and thin, whether it be helping me through a panic attack, or celebrating the smallest of successes. I love you guys!! Thanks to SummerTech Computer Camps and Steve for being my first computer science family—*Tampon Run* would not have existed if you guys didn't give me the coding foundation and support and looove during the two summers I spent at Fort Awesome. The Hunter College High School community deserves a special shout-out for being so accommodating while I wrestled with balancing schoolwork and *Tampon Run* obligations. Especially Mr. Young for telling me he was proud of me after my TEDx talk—it meant a lot! And of course, I'd like to thank Sophie for being the best partner-in-crime I could have had. I could not have made it this far without your eloquence, humor, and unlimited access to your fridge. I couldn't imagine going on this journey with anyone but you!

SOPHIE:

Thank you to my parents and my brothers. You are endlessly supportive and you have taught me to value the weird. And Mom, as much shit as we give you, you are a great mom and I love you. You inspire me to always speak up, to always self-advocate, and I hope to be as much of a badass, strong woman as you are. Thank you to Lilly, Michal, and Simone. The "farts in room (mansion?)" that saw in me what I didn't always see in myself. And to Clem, my #lp, who was there from day one in her dorm room when I put the phone down and said "I'm writing a book . . . ?" to right at this moment as I write these acknowledgments across from you to literally every moment of my life in between. You all, and the rest of my incredible friends, make life beautiful and inspire me endlessly. I would not be who I am today without all of you. To Andy, for making this ridiculous journey fun and funny. I've been so lucky to have you to my right (never to my left) every step of the way. And, lastly, to my teachers and the administration at Bard High School Early College where I learned to think and to question. You were all so encouraging and understanding when *Tampon Run* turned my life upside down.